# THE MISADVENTURES OF
# A JILTED JOURNALIST

## JUSTIN LITTLE

Copyright © 2018 by Justin Little

Cover by Matthew Revert

ISBN: 978-1-944866-25-9

Non-Fiction/Essays

CLASH Books: Part of The YESCLASH! Series #1

PO BOX 487 Claremont, NH 03743

"Sometimes the first duty of intelligent men is the restatement of the obvious."

— GEORGE ORWELL

# CONTENTS

# INTRODUCTION

## By Autumn Christian

This morning I woke up inside of a miracle.

I pulled on my mass-produced clothing, walked into my air-conditioned kitchen, and opened a refrigerated box powered by an electrical grid that covered the entire city. I grabbed a bottle of iced coffee that was created in a factory with millions of others and shipped to my local grocery store through a mass distribution network. Then I headed over to my office in the back of the house, where I powered on a box that is hooked up to a network that has the entire recorded history of the human race inside of it. (If the Macedonians had the Internet, the Library of Alexandria would've been burned down a lot faster.)

Then I scrolled down my Twitter feed to find that the human race was doomed.

Nazis are marching on Washington — again.

Donald Trump is about to start nuclear war.

Racists are destroying black America.

Alex Jones has been banned from YouTube, which simultaneously means that free speech is dead, and that our children are finally safe.

People still need clean water in Flint.

Guns either need to be banned, or need to be more freely available — and either way our freedom is at stake.

Laura Ingalls Wilder's name was stripped from a children's book award to protect minority children from racism. The endless debate over how many genders there are and what means for society, diversity, and oppression, continues to wage.

Also I think it's Mercury Retrograde again, so something terrible is about to come hurling at us from the astral plane, and all our electronics are going to break at once.

Repeat these exchanges on YouTube, Facebook, Snapchat, Reddit, News aggregator sites, the dinner table, the break room at work, and any other place where humans gather in both small and large groups.

I imagine the exchanges going back and forth like soldiers slinging grenades across barbed wire. Someone gets banned. A bomb detonates. People limp away from an onslaught of trolls, clutching empty space where their limbs used to be.

And that's not a terribly inaccurate view — studies have suggested that we react to facts that go against our worldview much the same as a physical threat. Our pulse goes up. Adrenaline starts pumping. Our vision narrows. Because to us, our worldview is life.

It is the thing that informs our every motion and movement. It is the road that we walk upon to continue to try to survive.

It can be difficult to parse through all the noise and chaos (Which, thanks to the Internet, is expanding by the second), to know when to respond and when to recede, to know what to focus our energy on, and what's bullshit and what isn't. To know where we're heading, and what's an illusion. Especially when, for most of us, our day to day life does not reflect the inchoate static of global violence and invisible infrastructures of oppression. We exist in cool interiors, have to deal with daily minor annoyances while sipping Starbucks lattes, and only see violence and extreme pain in rare, singular instances.

But the answer to our problems have always been the same.

It's the answer that helped us hunt down the mammoths, learn how to create fire, and cook them over roaring pits. It's what brought us from the abyss of non-existence to hospitals, air-conditioned airports, and science labs. It is both extraordinarily simple, and endlessly complicated. It is an answer that is also a question.

What is truth?

Because to quote Justin Little in the essay from this book, "The truth exists regardless of how we feel about it. The truth never goes away, and all overly sensitive people can do is force you to not acknowledge it."

Justin Little is like an electric knife of light that cuts smoothly through the darkness.

A journalist who, like many who search for truth, has been jilted by those who have stakes in ideologies that regard them as irrelevant. A writer who has tasked himself with diving into the depths of inconsistencies, half-truths, snarling partisanship, and corporate distractions, to try to find the gleaming center of reality.

Justin Little is one of the people throughout history who have looked around and gone, "What the fuck is *actually* going on here?" and then went out to find the answer.

Not only because he recognizes how vitally important finding the truth is to the continued survival of our civilization, but because he's the kind of person who probably wakes up in the middle of the night with his brain burning, unable to rest until he's found it.

Justin writes about everything to the difference between the 1960s civil rights movements and our current protests, to Hunter Thompson's Gonzo journalism, to the way that Margaret Atwood's *The Handmaid's Tale* falls short of being the apocalyptic warning it purports to be, to a night with Jordan Peterson and how chaos affects our daily lives. Through every essay runs that same thread of parsing through the bullshit, of realizing that things are rarely as they appear, of a cynicism propelled by the pain of being an idealist.

His style is smooth and dry, like a whiskey that goes down

smooth. When Justin writes something like, "Hardly anyone fights for peace. Genuine peace. They all fight to be at the helm of peace. Controlled peace," with what feels like the calm and measured tone of a man narrating a nature documentary, the burn that follows the taste is almost pleasurable.

He's engaging and straight-forward, with an intelligent vocabulary that never falls into being erudite. And his use of New Journalism, in which the writer's story becomes a part of the thing he is reporting on, shows how all these disparate threads of ideas are connected — that these essays are not concerned with something taking place out in a distant land, but are an exploration of a vital part of what it means to be human. It is the kind of writing that "Told you everything while appearing to tell you nothing at all." Instead of being prescriptive, it's immersive. And it's in those immersive stories that we learn how ideas seep down into the microstructures of our lives and inform the smallest of our actions.

That is what truth is. It is both the macro and the micro. It is the infinite and the singular moment. It is what at every level and angle of exploration, does not fall apart.

We are constantly at war with ideas, and those ideas result in very real, actual violence. There are many people out there who get lost in the haze of untruth and those who want to make sure others stay lost. And it can become frightening to wonder where we're going, or if we're going to never get there, because we'll eat ourselves from the inside out.

Justin Little says the answer rests in truth. And not just truth, but the willingness to search for it. "All of us must face reality. Fear a little slower, and Loathe a little less. No one person can carry this burdensome torch, but all of us can try our best to make sure that the dim flickering flame it carries never ceases to light the end of the tunnel."

Me — I'm not too worried about the future of our species, because I have Chipotle and a Red Bull and a computer to type this introduction, the result of 200,000 or more years of truth-seeking and parsing reality from nonsense. Because people like Justin Little exist, who want to make the world a better place — not with tyrannical order, but with uncontrolled peace. Who are always willing to delve into the chaos, to "put themselves through the ringer and come out with a story on the other side," and find beauty in the truth they find.

# THE SIXTIES MILLENNIAL

Sometimes those of us who are stricken with the crippling weight of self-awareness fall into a state of obsessive self-critique. Unfortunately, I consistently occupy this territory. It affects my ability to confidently do my work without stressing myself out over lingering doubts I may have about the content in general, to include the quality of the writing and presentation therein. I thought it may be of use to flesh out one of those internal struggles. It might help another politically charged millennial examine themselves provided they hear something that they can relate to.

What brought on this period of inward analysis was a recent visit to the JFK Museum and Library. After I had waded through annoying school children who only enjoyed being there because it was a decent break from the usual crushing tedium that is the education system, I was able to get a good look at the biography of John F. Kennedy, some private tapes concerning the Cuban Missile Crisis, and a decent picture of a couple of the largest protest movements in United States history. Those two being the Civil Rights Movement, and protests against the war in Vietnam. It was an incredibly politically volatile decade, and one can't help but draw connections to the bubbling atmosphere that surrounds us at present.

I view most modern protests with an air of disdain, and fear looking back on this decade in my life disappointed with myself like many people did decades after the era of the 1960's admitting that they should've taken the grievances more seriously. Many eventually admitted that the government and military *had* been systemically murderous during the Vietnam War after all (much of this is detailed in Nick Turse's book "Kill Anything That Moves"), and that the abolition of slavery didn't prevent Black Americans in the South from being forced into second class citizenship under the law in the form of various discriminatory policies. Although, some who partic-ipated in the protests of the 60's look back in disappointment for other reasons. They view their activities as naïve and were they to do it all over again they wouldn't have been as viciously strident. Perhaps they would've condemned some of the violent tendencies within their own camp in harsher terms. Maybe they would've been more agreeable when it came to compromise. One hears phrases such as those frequently.

Just recently I've realized that condemning myself to a life as a political lone wolf may not have been the correct decision, and I should get more involved in the real world regarding what I find to be important. Instead of just writing pieces about them, brushing my hands off, and thinking that my work here is done. As of right now, part of me thinks that I wasted many of my turbulent years critiquing a kind of feigned rebelliousness. While the other part of me thinks that this faux-revolutionary attention seeking behavior is a poison when it comes to genuine dissent in the face of a deluded majority and that makes it all worth it in the end.

A cultural status quo that pretends to buck the system in order to maintain itself is not an oppositional force in the slightest. It's a movement of narcs acting in a manner that they perceive serious contrarian activists are supposed to be acting. I can't bring myself to treat many flavors of the modern day activist with the same kind of seriousness that left-wing activists in the 60's deserve to be treated with.

The modern American has become a loyal companion to betrayal. As if it is always an understandable act of pragmatic need by their candidate of choice. In the recesses of their minds they must know that the promises on offer will not be completed for whatever reason. I refuse to believe that human memory only spans eight years. Whether it's the candidate going back on their word for cynical personal gain, or the various checks other portions of the government have on word keeping. One imagines this would prevent the presidential candidate from making promises they are unsure whether they can keep, but declining promising results is probably the worst thing a candidate can do for their image, despite how true it may be. Realistic promises aren't exciting but anything raucously declaring "Change," "Strength," "Unity," or some monumental political overhaul are effective. Vague words said powerfully are more energizing than specific words said tenu-ously. The knife being stabbed into the backs of the American population doesn't cause pain anymore, and hardly needs to crawl through flesh. That wound becomes a necessary human mutation. It begins to feel the same as turning a key, or shoving a quarter into a coin slot.

The sixties are revered by many in the modern era because it symbolizes the rejection of that kind of mentality. Not only a rejection of the generic establishment, but a rejection of the idea that it has always been, is always, and will always be a hopeless scenario. Diving into a comfortable form of cold apathetic cynicism which boasts of a hard outer shell, but secretly wishes it could see a brighter future. The devilishly cartoon face of Richard Nixon being almost a perfect oppo-nent snuck into history by some ethereal novel writer that thought to introduce an antagonist a bit later in the timeline. Looking back through history, the 60's seemed to be a perfect synthesis of optimism and dissident passion. That's why so many in the 2010s are doing their very best to replicate it, but have failed miserably in every attempt thus far.

THE FIRST STOP ON MY TOUR OF THE JFK LIBRARY AND Museum led me through a few glass cases featuring some JFK related objects. His high school report card (in which his grades were worse than your humble author's), the crutches he used when dealing with an injury, and a paper on World War II British mobilization that he wrote as a thesis in college. The lower level is where I headed next, the entrance to which makes the visitor feel like they're sneaking past the guards into a secret wing of the Museum itself. This brought me to a hallway spattered with Presidential Election paraphernalia. JFK and Nixon buttons were on display.

Both of my ears were immediately assaulted with different election speeches. I wonder whether this was intentional, but such a feature would apply more to the 2010s than the 1960s. The present is the age of non-stop information. We live in an age where our technology gives the average citizen the opportunity to search for needed information with minimal effort. However, the dark underbelly of this convenience means that those wishing to spread disinformation have all of that convenience at their fingertips as well. Citizens in the 60s had naught but their static laden televisions and radios.

You cannot speak to a politician through a television, but you can speak to them (or more appropriately, speak at them) through social media like Facebook and Twitter. One can even organize a mass internet-based protest. What isn't taken into account is, as soon as politicians turn off their computers all proper dissent given to them through this medium, vanishes into virtual non-existence. This is why physical political action should still be valued more highly than social media *cough* "activism." Of course that all depends on what is being protested, and how it is being protested, but we'll get to that a little bit later.

Social media has influenced us to an unhealthy degree. This is what many, I'm sure, wrote about the radio and television. So it's not a unique insight, really. Strolling down the adjoining hallway led me to bright matte colors and round-edged home appliances. Clearly trying with all of their might to force the museum-goer to picture themselves in an apron. Once you pass by these incredibly interesting household items you're greeted with a booth displaying part of the first televised Presidential debate between John F. Kennedy, and Richard Nixon.

The lazy-eyed upturned face of JFK and the sweaty, jittery, and awkward laughing Nixon have a debate that is (while dull) surprisingly substance based. There are jabs back-and-forth, but much effort is made by both candidates to remain respectful and condemn the ideas of the man, not the man. Almost to a sneer-inducing degree. Even when it was unnecessary Nixon would ask JFK to acknowledge that his own words were sincere, and compliment JFK on the sincerity of his words. Perhaps a pathological insecurity of Nixon's knowing internally that many of his words were not? Maybe. Maybe not.

The debate was supposed to be focused on fiscal domestic policy, but this was inevitably related to the Cold War where JFK appeared to take a harder line on Communism. Mainly due to Nixon doing his best to stick to defending the Republican Party's domestic record. Not to say that JFK necessarily maintained a stronger opinion about international Communism than Nixon, but Nixon didn't put his foot down as intensely as JFK did during this particular debate. The backdrop of the argument was a dull light grey color due to everything in the picture being black and white. Far different from the air raid siren of colored and reflective prisms given to us during modern electoral debates. The intensity of the setting is inversely correlated to how much substance is present. While there may not have been a "golden age" of anything, one must admit that the 60s were at the very least, a tad shinier where it mattered. It's like comparing a diamond to cubic zirconium. To the untrained eye it's easy to view them both as identical, but only one has any real value beneath the distracting shimmer.

⚜

MY EVER-PERSISTENT CYNICISM HAS CONVINCED ME THAT we're dealing with a cheap imitation of politics. As if everyone at the same time agreed to put on a sleazy charade. I do my best to beat back that mentality though because a young jaded solipsist is one of the worst types of people to listen to. Genuine movements do still exist. It's possible that they are just rarer specimens. Part of me thinks the job of political pundit has ascended to the level of pop-star or famous actor in desirability amongst young people. With everyone viewing themselves as something of a master analyst comes an unfortunate lowering of our cultural standards for what is considered biting and insightful commentary. To partly plagiarize Christopher Hitchens, "Everyone's got an opinion in them, but much of the time, that's where it should stay." Not to elevate myself to any arrogant position, I do my best to shut my mouth when I don't know what I'm talking about.

A lesson the political and journalistic professions (but alas I repeat myself) should take heed of. Viewing a couple of panel discussions on any old or new media platform will do this convincing for me. All of the power and influence is captured and stowed away by the charismatic, narcissistic, and insecure. This happened because of humanity's tendency to grant intellectual legitimacy, job opportunities in the political sphere, and cash on the basis of victimization instead of the quality of one's ideas and insights.

Being victimized is a fast track to political stardom in our culture, which is why one sees so much sinister exaggeration of victimhood, or people cynically facilitating their own victimization in order to feign shock about it. No story gives credence to my theory regarding victimization and political stardom more than the quickly organized cult of David Hogg. He is a testament to this theory of mine, but this can be applied to some right-wing pundits as well (the greasy image of Laura Loomer springs to mind immediately).

It developed into personality worship considering CNN began to talk about how much of a travesty it was that Hogg was rejected from various colleges that he applied to. Hopefully they will report on when and if he gets a new girlfriend too. This kid is no expert on anything apart from what it's like to be a victim, but is paraded around as if he's some brand new mind on the scene saying new things that none of us have heard before. He says things consistent with a moderately intelligent high school freshman's understanding of Civics, nothing he is saying hasn't already been better expressed, it's not like we haven't heard every single one of his arguments surrounding gun policy before, and getting needlessly tender over his words or my critique of him will not disabuse us of this uncomfortable fact. The emotional devastation of a school shooting will have a strong effect on whoever is unfortunate enough to experience it, but if one wants to enact lasting political change, one must do more than play tug of war with heartstrings. The reason a pathetic foundation of sycophants began raising up David Hogg is because of his victim status. That's it. There is something innately creepy about grown adults idolizing a teenager too, and perhaps that goes to show just how infantilized the American population has become.

What bothers me the most about this tendency to reward victims with political clout is the contempt it shows for the revolutionary attitude. As if revolution, dissent, rebellion, distrust of authority, and all of these valuable things are just another commodity that's paid lip-service to so long as it can be capitalized on for short-term gain. How many media personalities market themselves on their bucking of the system and the status quo? There comes a time when one has to ask the question: "Is the status quo pretending to be a revolutionary force?"

Might sound a bit conspiratorial to some, but if one considers the Women's March and the Hogg-friendly "MarchForOurLives" protests" one can readily see the insincerity present within both. The shutting down of speakers over their "associations" "implications" and "harmful rhetoric" is practically bursting with McCarthyist undertones. Compare these protests to the ones in Selma, Alabama. People being defleshed by fire hoses. To sit-ins. To Vietnam War protests. To the demanding of Free Speech by students at Berkeley in the mid-1960s. Fighting for freedom of expression, the end of government mandated discrimination against black people, the demand to end a war that was declared to be winding down right before the Tet Offensive happened in 1968.

Dissent is an absolute farce now compared to then. It's become more about saying things than doing things. Maximum optics for minimal effort. Half-assed talking points easily rebutted by someone who took a 101 course on the subject. Filled to the brim with people who know nothing, but claim to understand everything. They are forgetting that dissent is not merely body mobilization and the ability to put on a good well-covered rally. It needs to have intellectual heft to it as well. It lacks this because the population has become either too willing to forgive outright stupidity for the sake of political expediency, or the population has become too dumb to notice. Both the Civil Rights Movement and the protests against the War in Vietnam had solid arguments they could build a movement out of. Many present-day "rebels" are trying to build a roof on a house with no walls, and it shows.

This is due to the left-wing becoming too comfortable being the cultural consensus within many parts of the United States. Though, the right still has a stranglehold on some parts of the country primarily in the South. The consensus is different depending on where one travels, but moral indignation has become the bedrock of argument in almost every sphere including government. I think there's a mass eye-roll that's getting larger and larger whenever a politician attempts to sleaze their way into our emotions instead of appealing to the brain of the American citizen.

I suppose I can't tell which is the cause and which is the effect in relation to the apparent dumbing down of the American citizenry, at least in the political realm. This could be too harsh of me, because I do recognize a bias within me to support the underdog. For example if I were residing within an area of the United States where the generic right held consensus I'd be doing my best to force them to deal with my left-wing beliefs, the same goes for an area that has a generic left-wing consensus. If there is anything I do hold dear, it is defending positions I hold for which there is no comfortable majority to rest in. Which is a bias I have to deal with when examining history and coming to conclusions on issues of rebellion and mass dissent.

AFTER YOU EXIT THE DEBATE BOOTH AND WALK PASSED JFK giving his inaugural address, you enter a long hallway dolled up to look like you're inside the White House. An interesting experience if I do say so myself. As someone who will most likely never see the inside of the White House personally it was fun to live vicariously through a replica for a few seconds.

There were gifts given to Kennedy by various leaders of other countries lining the walls. A small room dedicated to space exploration, and an interactive mock press conference where I was challenged to take the role of President and answer questions about policy from reporters (after being given a few briefs to read). It turns out I answered with about a 50-50 split between Kennedy's answers, and the answers of progressive radicals during that time period. It eased my mind a bit when it came to which side I would be on if I lived during this time, but then again I remembered that I wouldn't have had this time period to look back on for advice were I living in that very time period.

It is often said in a disapproving tone by those who wish to cast some shady eyes at 60s activists that they were heavily associated with Socialists and Communists, and that is indeed partly true. It might be said that some of the opposition to the Vietnam War was motivated by the desire to see Communism spread, however, this does not preclude that any motivation behind opposition to the Vietnam War was improper or devious in nature. From everything I've read I've been shown that Marxist and Socialist membership was growing within student populations. It should be noted though that this is the same fear tactic given today surrounding free speech movements consistently bringing up in a very sly purposeful way that these free speech people are heavily associated with the far-right— yes, geniuses, free speech activists tend to associate with those having their speech suppressed —you've cracked the case.

I patiently waited for around ten minutes wandering the hall for a short 15-20 minute movie to play, which showcased the internal workings of the President's Cabinet during the Cuban Missile Crisis. Complete with intelligence photographs of the missile sites garnished with Kennedy arguing with his contemporaries about whether or not to invade Cuba. As we all know the Bay of Pigs occurred before this incident, and Kennedy was looking to avoid another disaster like that. They have an entire section of the Library based around Kennedy's failure which surprised me a bit. I thought it would just be Kennedy praise the whole time. It's reasonable to assume that they knew they couldn't skip such a large section of history.

Then we are greeted with JFKs address regarding Civil Rights that he delivered to the American people on June 11th, 1963. A great victory for its time. However, now we HAVE the Civil Rights Acts of '57, '60, and '64 which outright makes illegal these types of bigoted practices. Yes, there was a piece of legislation drawn up in the 50s, but when discussing "The 60s" as a decade, it's important to mention things that happen from the 1950s all the way until the early 1970s. To put it bluntly, modern progressives are fighting battles that have already been won for them. To exclude things like the gay marriage issue. The fight to prevent minorities from being considered second class citizens under the law has been won already. Women have the vote with strong cultural and Constitutional bulwarks against their rights being curtailed. Progressives are foolishly spending their time debating whether or not their political opponents should be allowed the right to speak freely as opposed to making their arguments any stronger. It can be safely said that if a faction of politics is publicly debating the value of free speech for their opponents without soul-crushing embarrassment, they have at least won culturally. They are stomping through already conquered legal ground as if the enemy still controls the territory and think that they (on some mental level) deserve credit in the history books for being the honorary generational heir to that throne.

Unfortunately for them it's become a practice in adopting something of a religious fervor in their language (discounting of course Martin Luther King's distinct references to Christian themes in speeches). Not religious in the sense that it references God, but religious in the sense that it is a type of adopted language that one must learn before one can produce informed speech on social issues. There's a necessary moral attitude that one must express to be considered "left wing" that many do not or cannot hold to. The cultural standards for what can be properly labeled "left wing" are becoming stricter and stricter, and people are treated to a kind of "political one-drop rule" when it comes to left-wing and right-wing.

Believe that gay people should be allowed to get married, believe that climate change is real, believe that wealth should be redistributed in some fashion, think minorities get a bad deal in modern society, believe that the welfare state should be expanded, believe in internationalism as opposed to national- ism, believe that we should open the borders, oh...but you think that abortion is a moral wrong? Sorry, not left wing, not pure enough, you're now a right-winger who is in opposition to women's rights. Then everyone puts their hands on their heads and wonders where in the world all these right-wingers and apathetic people came from.

I'm unsure as to whether things like this happened in the 60s when people were trying to mobilize mass support for causes, but I can only assume if it did it was on a much less extreme scale. If you were opposed to the Vietnam War, come on down and support. If you were in favor of Civil Rights legislation, come on down and march with us. It was about the cause, and enacting real lasting political change, not a sideshow act where a left-winger sits on a self-made throne judging whether each applicant is left-wing enough to be asso- ciated with. I did hear stories like this about drug culture in the 60s though. That left-wingers who refused to take mari- juana or psychedelics were considered not "really part of the cause man" but that was the extent of it.

The progressive has tainted its stellar legacy over the past decade. It submitted itself to a sickly combination of guilt-ridden flagellating and a non-stop stress ridden purity test. In my experience, it seems like the majority of people who get to be taken seriously by mainstream outlets have agreed to participate in this for the sake of still being viewed as left wing in the eyes of their social media peanut gallery comrades. The 60s Millennial is inundated with passion over mundane things. One example of this being Justin Trudeau's proposal a few months ago to change the official Canadian National Anthem for the purpose of it having "gender neutral language" and claimed that this was another step on the road to gender equality.

If someone truly believed that women were oppressed in the nation of Canada, which I don't, this looks like a condescending waste of time doesn't it? Yes women, we progressives are totally on board with the whole gender equality thing and you shouldn't be oppressed anymore, so here, we changed the national anthem so it doesn't say the word "sons" anymore. I have to ask whether they're fucking joking.

What I don't understand is why so many find it difficult to figure out why someone would willingly protest and march with 60s radical progressives regarding social policy, and then march with right-wingers in the 2010s over issues of free speech. It's the principle of the thing. Being a supporter of the Civil Rights Movement in the 60s, and being a supporter of modern right-wing free speech movements is not contradictory. It's simply consistent with someone who believes that both of those movements should be successful in persuading the government (or the general culture) to change their attitude on a particular issue. The fact that it might be a predominantly left wing or right wing movement doesn't factor into it, or at least it shouldn't if one is being true to themselves instead of being true to peer pressure. Maybe I'm not the one who put myself in a political lone wolf scenario here. Maybe I'm just not pure enough to have a comfortable political home. Why would anyone want one?

I EXITED THE BUILDING AFTER BROWSING A ROOM SET UP TO look like Robert Kennedy's office. I left the building with a sense of uncertainty in myself and a kind of renewed political vigor. It jolted me out of my previous biases, and handed me some beautiful historical perspective.

The main difference between the 60s protests and modern protests is the overall strength of the thing being protested. The persecution of minorities is not as strong as it had been, and very few are in favor of their persecution in the present. While it does still happen it isn't nearly on the scale that it used to be. There's been an embracing of victimhood as a desirable personal trait as opposed to it being something that must be overcome. The "white and bigoted" segment of American politics is laughably small. In the sixties you had an army of citizens that were sick of being trampled on throwing the boots off of their backs and the backs of others. Today we're seeing the mere cultural bullying of the weakest fringes of the political landscape, or more accurately, those that have been dishonestly defined into those fringes. It is brave and eye-watering to see people demanding their government recognize their freedom. My eyes don't exactly mist over when I see thousands of millennials railing against something that is, in a pragmatic sense, already politically dead. Yet they choose to keep it alive through a frightening form of mass hallucination.

We have people in the mainstream news and in new media that don't fall within the fringes constantly patting themselves on the back over how they aren't insane like racial nationalists, and violent political fringes without having any actual discussion, presenting any new ideas, or even referencing the topic at hand. We congratulate one another over how reasonable we are and how we are able to have a conversation without actually having the conversation! And dear lord Almighty if you're patting yourself on the back for not being a proto-Fascist or a Communist, and being stable enough to have a polite discussion with someone that's basically like giving yourself a gold star for not pissing all over the toilet seat at thirty-two years old.

Having the ability to have a political discussion and not be a nutjob requires knowing barely more than jack squat. You can only "demolish snowflakes" or "own the Trumpsters" so many times before people start wondering what else you're good for and too often we discover that the answer to that question is nothing. People know just enough to hold their own in an argument with the stupidest people on the planet, and act like that makes them the next coming of Christopher Hitchens or Carl Sagan. We've gotten to a point where instead of ignoring the crazy people, we spend all of our time obsessing over how stupid and crazy they are to the point where some think it's a good idea to give them the attention they desperately want by sic'ing the government or the latest offense prevention agency on social media platforms on them, pumping up their victim cred, and having them be reported on in main-stream news letting every similar crazy person know that there's a movement for them too.

I am constantly crippled by how much I don't know. It takes me days to muster up the courage to write down an Op-Ed piece for fear that I messed up some minor detail because I don't want to be lazy. I don't want to unintentionally lie to my audience. When I see people who know nothing about pretty much everything getting guest spots on popular news networks getting to spread their ideas around because they are either complete idiots that the host wants to make fun of, they were victimized by idiots and are seizing the opportunity, or they made up their victimization altogether.

It makes me wonder whether I've been going about this whole "writer" business wrong and I should become a glorified political prankster so I can be exalted by a bunch of opportunists as the next great mind of our time. We like to think that the time we are living in is normal, but I don't think it is. I can feel the tide of history turning, but I can't make out which direction we're going in to be perfectly honest. But I feel the tug.

I suppose latent in all of us is the fear that thirty years from now we will be the uptight dusty grey conservative who opposed the things that history now deems righteous. Maybe I'm searching for perfection in a world that doesn't contain it. Maybe I do just need to take a risk, bulldoze over my doubts and the doubts of others. I always thought that doubt was a virtue, and in many ways it is, but it can also become a ball and chain if one has too much of it. What do they say about too much of a good thing? The rebellious spirit is being commoditized which dilutes it. The psychological fringes in our society are being emboldened by sensationalism.

I could be romanticizing the past, I probably am. Maybe we romanticize the past because it gives us hope that a better future is possible. I think that's why I enjoy radical writers more than I do those in the center. The center is very keen on "making the best of a bad situation" while more radical writers want to believe that the bad situation can be turned into a good one. Everybody wants to save the world in one sense or another, but every single event just catapults us further down to the rock bottom conclusion that the world doesn't want to be saved. Maybe it doesn't need saving right now.

I've reached the unfortunate conclusion that hardly anyone fights for peace. Genuine peace. They all fight to be at the helm of peace. Controlled peace. Perhaps that's the only way us humans can be peaceful is if we're forced into it. But, for some reason, on a visceral level, there's something beautiful about fighting for uncontrolled peace. Where everyone can be okay with each other's existence without the disingenuous help of some higher authority. Whenever there is a spark of uncontrolled peace, those who control the current peace stomp it out. Making sure to asphyxiate it. Because it was never about the acquisition of peace. It was always about the control.

They conflate peace and order and they always will. What needs to be shown to the mass of political control freaks isn't that we have the ability to crush them physically or outmaneuver them politically. It's that we are perfectly capable of bringing about peace without their help. I suppose that's the problem with being an idealist, internally you know that you'll never reach the places you think should be reached. All you can do in life is try to make the world slightly better while your contemporaries try their hardest to make it slightly worse.

The future, I predict, is going to be one where you are a little more docile, a little squishier, a little more regimented, slowly bled of your individuality for the sake of some grand vision, and it's likely that you'll love every minute of it.

I know I'm being vague, but maybe it's time to look at the big picture. I'm not saying that everything is terrible, or everything is dumb, because it isn't. It's just shallow. It's shallow because we made it shallow. Erdogan, China removing term limits, Assad, North Korea, The Kurds, Putin, the oppression in Burma, the horrors in South Africa. The plight of millions of oppressed people ignored in favor of cracking down on casual bigotry. People punching one another for speaking without their permission in the United States and UK. The psychological fringes of our society being stoked by sensationalism to the point where they decide to shoot their political opponents. Run them over with cars. Throw fireworks at them. Play at being proponents of peace while engaging in the only version of war they are brave enough to undertake. Dignity, compassion and reason are not winning in the 2010s. At this rate they never will, but the idealist in me has to believe that they could one day. If I didn't believe that I don't think I would've made it to twenty-four.

# THE VALUE OF GONZO

I've said before that life is a constant struggle between your inner hippie and inner soldier. Hunter S. Thompson said "screw it" and decided to be both. It is often said that great minds discuss ideas, average minds discuss events, and small minds discuss people. However, all of these concepts intersect in some variety or another. Ideas come from people, events are organized by people, events are organized around an idea, ideas contribute to the behavior of people. Not to say it's a useless quotation, but there are occasions where great minds should discuss people.

Hunter Thompson is credited with inventing "Gonzo Journalism" although journalists had been partaking in this particular method before he existed. Ernst Junger being one example of this, writing of his experiences in the trenches during World War One. Ernest Hemingway and Jack London were also practitioners of this form. Thompson didn't so much invent the concept as much as he put a name to the method. Gonzo Journalism. As someone who has been a frequent proponent of objective journalism it was interesting immersing myself in the work of Hunter S. Thompson, a man who had a lot of scorn for objective journalism in his time.

Instead of trying to make a case for objective journalism in opposition to Thompson, I decided to use Hunter's Gonzo style on himself using a process called "method reading." Which involved diving into the Studs Terkel Radio archive listening to old interviews with Thompson, reading biographies about him, watching documentaries about his life, picking up his mannerisms, his style of dress, his speaking cadence, and inflicting myself on the terrified unfortunate denizens of the Boston area. To truly live the story and become part of it for this piece I had to embody the spirit of Hunter S. Thompson himself.

If I'm going to let a writer influence me, I prefer to let myself get all the way under the influence. It inspired me to write this piece on Hunter S. Thompson, his life, lessons to be learned from him, and how we should be applying his attitude to the 21st Century.

As someone with a mild interest in the profession of journalism I'd always heard the name Hunter S. Thompson thrown around. I had heard of journalists who tried to imitate his style of "Gonzo journalism," but due to their miserable failures I'd dismissed the concept entirely as an excuse for lazy journalism. This is one of those rare instances where I will readily admit just how wrong I was. Not in the sense that many people try and fail to practice Gonzo journalism, but that it was a completely useless method used to fluff the egos of bad journalists. Frequently during my rants about objectivity I would get one or two of his quotations thrown my way in rebuttal, and decent rebuttals they were.

I've always been a reader who works author by author. Getting entrenched in a writer's style and outlook on life appeals to me much more than jumping story to story, style to style. The thought of going from a Hemingway novel to something of Faulkner's was horrific to me. I decided to get started with "The Rum Diary." Thompson wrote this novel when he was twenty-two, kept it in a trunk for decades after it got rejected over and over again, then got it published back in 1998. I kept it simple by going to a bar, ordering a few rum and cokes, and read it as intensely as I could force myself to do.

I was immediately captivated by the gritty beauty of his prose. It was a comforting departure from all of the prim and proper political reading I'd been doing, and this moment was the start of a relaxing incline out of my political obsessions. As I was reading about these journalists in Puerto Rico getting into all sorts of shenanigans, fighting with their publishers, and indulging in poisonous amounts of drink, I looked up from the novel to the television hanging on the wall.

The screen featured some stuffed suit talking about the state of the American economy and how the President was either doing a fantastic job or failing the common man. It didn't really matter which opinion he had because his opinion was most likely dependent on his job description anyhow. I realized in that moment that I cared more about what happened to Paul Kemp in this Hunter S. Thompson novel than I cared about whatever some politician had to say about the economy. I began to feel contempt for all things official, or even official-looking, and I could feel the spirit of Thompson leaking into my soul.

Hunter S. Thompson was masterful at presenting the lifestyles of politicians and journalists in a way that people who were completely ignorant of these professions could understand. Both of these jobs are cloaked in jargon and lies, but getting to the grime of the whole ordeal was Thompson's specialty. There is a difference between a press release saying that a politician is "taking medication for sleep and stress related issues" or a Hunter S. Thompson description that would read something like: "He would snatch up a bottle of Adderall and down it like cheap beer after the flight, all the while still climbing out of a Xanax-induced nap. Such chemical clashes turned the candidate into a confused whack job for a couple hours after every airplane ride."

Both are true on their faces, but one of them seems truer because of the additional details, doesn't it? Plus the perception is different too, and arguably a more accurate perception of this fictional candidate can be drawn from the second line. But, of course, that second line would never make it past an editor concerned with objectivity and getting themselves sued. Hunter's writing style and truth-telling capacity was the exact opposite of your average White House press release and that's what I enjoyed about it. Press Releases are keen at telling you nothing while appearing to tell you everything. Hunter S. Thompson told you everything while appearing to tell you nothing at all.

It was at this moment I went all in with method reading Hunter S. Thompson. A few nights afterward I went to a bar and intended to play the part of Thompson before I dove further into his work, and an interesting weird night ensued. It was extra difficult for an introvert like myself to do this, but I did my very best. The night ended with a middle-aged woman buying me a double of Hennessey. This was followed by a slightly aggressive interrogation about whether or not I was Portuguese. I could tell she was completely in the bag due to her words coming out like she was gargling oatmeal, and the fact that she thought someone who looks like me might hail from a place that gets a lot of sun.

You can't help but introspect while you're playing the character of Thompson. While you're trying to focus on the fun and weirdness of everything the big questions start to seep through and they are always political and personal in nature. You never come up with a complex enough answer for yourself either, the answers are always simple and poorly thought through, but they sound right at the time. For example, I started thinking about superficiality in the 21st Century American character and couldn't help but connect it to the themes of Fear and Loathing in Las Vegas. At this point I'd only seen the movie.

I started thinking about how overcoming adversity is a dying action because so many of us are obsessed with removing all adversity from our lives and replacing it with positivity and unconditional support. The superficiality of all of this positivity and support gives the average person license to ignore their conscience or silence it completely. They don't have to volunteer at the soup kitchen because they shared a petition online about homelessness and hunger.

Our culture has evolved into a mass of tattletales desperately searching for the nearest authority figure, and we feel the most joy when we're filling out complaint forms. We're filled to the brim with people "completely willing to make a scene" acting in the role of "advocate of the people" when in reality they're just trying to get the 24-hour return policy extended for their lazy selves. There are certain things about the world that you can't learn from a textbook, or any kind of book for that matter. Hunter S. Thompson, while he attempts to describe these particular things in books, makes it clear that you'll never truly understand exactly what it's like to be punched in the face until it actually happens to you.

We are very keen on support, understanding, and positivity. But much of the time the support consists of unchecked validation, the understanding is superficial at best, and the positivity can get to one's head. Support, understanding, and positivity are good things but only when they're genuine and given after a horrific negative experience. When someone needs all of these things constantly in order to get through the suffering of life in general then they most likely have a chemical imbalance of some type. Either that or they are dreadfully narcissistic and need people telling them that they love them all the time.

The world can be described as two politicians in expensive suits arguing over a piece of bread while a homeless man starves directly in front of them. We've forgotten that we don't need to be public figures in order to help people. Engaging in illusory and ineffective political actions that deliver convenient excuses for why we behave poorly elsewhere, all the while maintaining the false belief that we're having a net positive effect on the world. A simple answer, probably wrong, but it sounds right in the moment.

I began diving into his material. I bought *Fear and Loathing in Las Vegas*, the book, and his collections, *The Great Shark Hunt* and *The Proud Highway* just to get a feel for him as a person. I watched every single documentary I could find on him, and unfortunately for Hunter nearly all of them treated him like some diseased exotic animal in a nature documentary. Always hovering around his front door waiting for him to do something, and unsure as to what might spook him. Desperately hoping he'll blow something up, shoot something, do something illegal, or be crazy and wacky in some fashion or another. It was sad really. If I were in that situation I'd feel like a dolphin being poked with a cattle prod and ordered to do tricks for the crowd.

The only two documentaries that treated him like a human being that I could find were *The Back Story of the Rum Diary* and *Breakfast with Hunter*. In a sense though, he cultivated this attitude toward him his whole life. Being a juvenile delinquent, doing a whole bunch of drugs, maintaining his outlaw status, constantly having run-ins with the police, saying provocative things, and all that jazz. Compare that persona to an author like Cormac McCarthy who has done like....one interview...and barely addresses the public at all.

His life is kind of a precursor to modern times especially in an age where more and more of the private life is becoming public knowledge thanks to the Internet. No matter the circumstance, people will treat you like you are the person you portray, not the person you are. Hence, why every actor, writer, CEO, politician, or whoever when they made a pilgrimage to Hunter S. Thompson's house expected him to be wild and crazy all the time. Much of this persona was amplified with his signature work, *Fear and Loathing in Las Vegas*. Thompson once remarked that this was a failed experiment testing out his method of Gonzo journalism. It was meant to be an exercise in treating the journalist's eyes and ears like a camera, writing everything down as he saw it happen, and then sending it in unedited for publication. A method that forces you to *become* the first person account of an event instead of being the person who interviews witnesses.

On a literary level it was vague search for the American Dream, where it has gone, and if it exists anymore. Of course, when the book came out and then the movie a long while after, new fans of his spawned a cult following that recreationally screamed about bats and did copious amounts of drugs. But in my opinion they were just buying into the tip of the Thompson iceberg when it came to this book. I think the most meaningful scene in the novel and movie is when he is whacked out on Adrenochrome, a drug that can only be extracted from a live human body, he can barely move, and the only thing he can see and hear is the image of Richard Nixon repeating the word "sacrifice" over and over again. It showed that Acid Culture in this time period was a form of escapism, and perhaps not the bastion of enlightenment and love that it was being advertised as.

He remarked on the drug culture as hopelessly optimistic. If one was moral, decent, and wore flowers in their hair then they will prevail. People were thinking they could, "buy Peace and Understanding for three bucks a hit." Despite all of that flower-power and love, there's always the dark underbelly of the people who made the drugs, sold them, fought over turf, and the violence and misery associated with that line of work. We still haven't learned these lessons. We still value this kind of superficiality. We all know precisely how to hate hatred, but we haven't quite figured out how to love yet. The American citizen is still succumbing to peer pressure. We feel the need to love in secret and hate in public, while professing that our hatred and disgust is coming from a place of love.

If one sentence could describe my generation it's the fact that we praise the hating of hatred more than we praise the loving of anything. Is it any wonder why everyone who even has a toe in the political game is so goddamned miserable all the time?

My favorite bit of writing from Hunter S. Thompson comes in the form of these paragraphs. From everything I've seen of Thompson, towards the end of his life it seemed like his biggest goal in life was writing something that was worth remembering like every writer does. This is one of the most memorable pieces of writing, to me, at least:

*"Strange memories on this nervous night in Las Vegas. Five years later? Six? It seems like a lifetime, or at least a Main Era—the kind of peak that never comes again. San Francisco in the middle sixties was a very special time and place to be a part of. Maybe it meant something. Maybe not, in the long run . . . but no explanation, no mix of words or music or memories can touch that sense of knowing that you were there and alive in that corner of time and the world. Whatever it meant. . . .*

*There was madness in any direction, at any hour. If not across the*

*Bay, then up the Golden Gate or down 101 to Los Altos or La Honda. .*
*. . You could strike sparks anywhere. There was a fantastic universal*
*sense that whatever we were doing was right, that we were winning. .*
*. .*

    *And that, I think, was the handle—that sense of inevitable victory*
*over the forces of Old and Evil. Not in any mean or military sense; we*
*didn't need that. Our energy would simply prevail. There was no point*
*in fighting—on our side or theirs. We had all the momentum; we were*
*riding the crest of a high and beautiful wave. . . .*
    *So now, less than five years later, you can go up on a steep hill in*
*Las Vegas and look West, and with the right kind of eyes you can*
*almost see the high-water mark—that place where the wave finally*
*broke and rolled back."*

It expresses a disillusioned idealist and optimist, finding
solace in drugs, in a depressed state over the fact that their
energy didn't prevail. It succumbed miserably to the same kind
of disingenuous superficiality present in politics, but that
doesn't mean that it shouldn't have happened. Let's just say
that someone like me can relate to that. There are deeper
themes in the life of Thompson that extend beyond "do drugs,
have fun, and buck authority" although those are important
parts of it. The lessons that can be learned from Hunter S.
Thompson are just as valuable now as they were a few decades
ago.

His work isn't a glorification of the hippie generation or
the Flower Power Activists, or extensive drug use, or hatred,
or anything like that. It was a criticism of American society,
and every American is a part of it whether they liked it or not.
There was a reason much of his work had "Fear and Loathing"
in the title. We're still addicted to those emotions. We believe
that Fear and Loathing only stem from other people, that they
don't reside quite comfortably within ourselves. He said as
much in an interview about the Hell's Angels and he talked
about how everyone has the capacity for violence and hatred,
but the people who function as "normal" bottle it up and
pretend it doesn't exist. Hunter S. Thompson was a huge
proponent of dealing with your own internal ugliness, and I
think that's something that is needed today. I suppose his

mindset and values apply just as well now as they did for generations passed.

Escapism is not the answer. Neither is paranoia or hatred. All of us must face reality, Fear a little slower, and Loathe a little less. No one person can carry this burdensome torch, but all of us can try our best to make sure that the dim flickering flame it carries never ceases to light the end of the tunnel.

# RUMINATIONS ON THE
# WRITER'S LIFE AND SUICIDE

"To be, or not to be," is the introduction to Shakespeare's most recognizable soliloquy and possibly the most famous monologue ever penned in the history of the writing profession. Just behind Hamlet, the second most well-known quotation about contemplating suicide comes from *The Myth of Sisyphus* by the French Absurdist Albert Camus which reads: "There is but one truly serious philosophical problem, and that is suicide." There's often a question looming over the minds of the public whenever a noteworthy artist takes their own life. Why do so many creative minds commit suicide?

Of course this question already has a bias built into it due to our focus on it. If sewage workers killed themselves at a rate higher than the average population I doubt our culture would consider it as serious a discovery and it's a shame they wouldn't. There is a massive amount of coverage whenever a famous person commits suicide, as evidenced by the self-inflicted death of Anthony Bourdain, and most of our famous people are either athletes or great successes in some form of artistic pursuit whether it be music, writing, acting, fashion design, directing, stand-up comedy, or film-making. Often cited is the refrain that it was the fame that killed them, for many artists are made for artistic creation, but their personalities aren't tailored to being a public figure or "household name."

Truly there can be no complete understanding as to the philosophical nature of why people kill themselves. There are indeed scientific explanations for this, and on occasion it can be helpful to those contemplating the act to view the internal strife they are experiencing as merely a chemical process, with the brain being so complex that it can more successfully fight its desire for death if it knows the process by which it makes war on itself. That has its limits though. Too frequently though is this overshadowed by the pain such a flooding of chemicals causes. If your hand gets lopped off with an axe, remembering the biological processes that send pain signals to the severed nerves doesn't dampen the anguish.

Ernest Hemingway, Hunter S. Thompson, Virginia Woolf, Yukio Mishima, possibly Jack London, and David Foster Wallace are all examples of writers that took their own lives, each one of them for their own reasons. Ernest Hemingway and Hunter S. Thompson both shot themselves. Virginia Woolf filled her clothes with rocks and marched herself into a river. Mishima committed seppuku after attempting a coup against the Japanese government. David Foster Wallace hanged himself from a rafter in his house. Every single one of these writers had different reasons for doing what they did, but most of them stem from mental illness. I've yet to find a case of someone who had no prior evidence of mental illness that "reasoned themselves into suicide," treating it like a pure intellectual exercise where death is a possible outcome, and if there are cases of this they are not here to explain their reasoning. Hence, why I think the statement by Camus is moot on this question.

There does seem to be an eternal relationship between authors, alcohol, and nicotine. Plenty of authors are heavy drinkers and smokers. There is no shortage of writers attempting to combat common mantras against excessive alcohol consumption. William Faulkner is known to have remarked: "My own experience has been that the tools I need for my trade are paper, tobacco, food, and a little whiskey." I don't mean to impede Faulkner's judgment, but one would assume that some sort of apparatus to transfer ink to page would be useful in this endeavor as well. Charles Bukowski once stated: "When you drank the world was still out there, but for the moment it didn't have you by the throat." A very emotional admission of using alcohol in order to deal with the sufferings of life. Neither of these men committed suicide though, unless the axiom that those who drink and smoke excessively actively intend to kill themselves at a slower pace is true. Those that abuse alcohol are more likely to commit suicide than those who don't, so perhaps it is the alcohol abuse that's at the root of this question? It isn't useful to get into the tobacco use because anyone who has tried both of these substances knows that alcohol alters your behavior and brain to a greater extent than tobacco does. Drink five whiskeys one evening, and then smoke five cigarettes the next and see for yourself which one has a greater effect on your inhibitions if you doubt my case.

At the intersection between alcohol and writers lies a mystery. Is it the job of writing that makes one lurch for the bottle, or is it the bottle that makes one stumble toward the keyboard? As most of us know alcohol lowers the inhibitions ensuring that you care less and less about what others think of you as the drinks slosh down your throat. The main issue writers have is a concept called "writer's block" which is an artsy term for "nothing I write is good enough for me." Alcohol has the effect of muting one's inner editor, because this internal character is built out of nothing but inhibition and insecurity.

There is a quintessential image of the "writer at work," which features a cigarette hanging out of the mouth, some sort of liquor in close proximity to the hands, and sternly staring at a typewriter. Despite our advances in technology the typewriter is what pops into people's heads when they imagine an author pounding through an unwritten section of their book. I often wonder whether this stereotype occurs naturally, or whether it's a self-perpetuating cycle of young upstarts trying their best to "fake it until they make it." Wisps of smoke fill the air; a sip of strong drink taken after every few "dings," and on the other side of this powerful session of work a master-piece is born. A perfectly acceptable evening, obviously, but what happens when alcohol doesn't just become a handy tool for writing when your inner editor is being extra harsh and instead becomes the foundation for the work?

If one's livelihood depends on getting meaningful words to print, and the only way one can do it is by drinking heavily, is it any wonder why so many writers succumb to the seductive allure of alcoholism? I don't mean to say that alcohol depen-dence is at the very core of why creative minds, authors in particular, kill themselves at what we think is a higher rate than the general population. As we've already detailed there are numerous contributing factors, but I don't think that alcohol dependence is a variable that should be overlooked if we're to examine the question honestly. Alcohol is not called a "depressant" for no reason. This is not intended to be a condemnation of the use of alcohol considering I drink enough of it myself to worry my physician. Christopher Hitchens has one of the most enlightening views on writing and drinking remarking that it is a, "good servant, but a bad master."

Leaving alcohol on the shelf for a minute, there is also a floating stereotype that writers must suffer to an enormous degree before they can start keying out quality words. I do find writing from a place of experience produces, on the whole, better and more honest work. George Orwell was a master at inflicting suffering on himself for the sake of his writing. The most well-known of these attempts is "Down and Out in Paris and London." He forces himself into poverty albeit with a rela-tively surefire way to get out of it at any time. However, one doesn't need the physical courage that Orwell possessed in order to produce honest first-person work either in the form of fiction or journalism. Depending on how dedicated one is to the art form and "the truth of the matter" there are other more minor examples of exemplary self-deprecation for the purposes of writing something worthwhile. In his early essay "Clink," Orwell attempted to discover what the British prison system was like so he got drunk, then slammed back a bunch of liquor in front of a couple of police officers in public. The trip ended in failure, however, as he was only kept in custody for forty-eight hours. While I cannot in any ethical capacity recommend this course of action, I will say that I admire that kind of journalistic dedication.

My point here is that many writers' lives can be treated as stories in and of themselves, and suicide is ultimately a "dramatic ending" for a life in a fictional story as well as the real world. It is possible however to intentionally live a captivating life, and write based on that experience, without having to put oneself through some kind of horrific ringer. No one's life is perfect. Everyone has hardships that they can draw from. Perhaps if your life has been overly extravagant, sheltered, and emotionally stable a quick trip to a homeless shelter or two would do some good to widen perspective. It would be easy for me to attempt to persuade the potential writer to avoid undue stress and anxiety in an effort to preserve their mental wellness.

If there are already mental issues plaguing you then try to keep it to a minimum. But for writers that are indeed mentally stable, there is nothing quite like launching yourself from a cannon until you fly an entire ocean away from your comfort zone. I still can't quite shake the feeling that writing is something one "lives" as opposed to something one "does." Perhaps for content writers on pop-up laden websites it's easy to churn out a thousand words on something completely insignificant and move on, but that of course is treating writing as a job one hates instead of something one "is." It is not difficult to get lost in the romanticism of the "writer's life," and eventually consider suicide to be a fitting end to the tale. Although I personally find suicide to be a lazy plot device when an author needs some loose ends tied up quickly.

F. Scott Fitzgerald, also a notorious heavy drinker, died thinking he was a complete failure considering his stories were only met with moderate attention. What would he think now that "The Great Gatsby" is taught in English curriculums across the United States as a shining beacon of American literature? My opinion on whether it should or shouldn't be taught notwithstanding, someone who holds an atheistic worldview considers this situation a travesty.

If there is one thing an artist lives for it is recognition. Even the most depressed, woe-is-me, and misanthropic writers have a burning desire for their art to be enjoyed despite the seething hatred for their own species and themselves. This common mantra is often said jokingly to the presently unsuccessful writer, "Well, we all know writers don't get famous until after they are dead." This is true in part because the drama of death is one of the most reliable inspirations to read somebody's thoughts. I even felt it myself when Tom Wolfe recently died. I had always "heard of him," but never "quite got into his stuff." I'm sure many of us have said this in reference to an artist's recent passing. In part this is due to praise-filled press coverage of said artist after their unfortunate demise. The mourning is cranked into overdrive if the artist took their own lives or died "in their prime."

Authors of great literary works will always have a complicated love-hate relationship with death; they sometimes tease it into coming to take them early through substance abuse and putting themselves in physical danger. Either that, or their inner demons win out after they've been fought long enough to put a satisfactory number of profound words to paper. There are numerous luminaries that died before my time, and I am desperate to ask them whether they would've had it any other way.

# GQ'S LITERARY FAILURE

Much profundity can be extracted from literature provided that one is not held down by literalism. It is often said that in order to competently perform in certain professions the "right kind of mind" must be possessed. Normally this is said about a field like computer science, but I find this is apt in describing literary critique as well. Perhaps not that a certain kind of mind must be possessed, but that a mind must not be preemptively sabotaged by the critic's obsession with contemporary politics, an inability to think abstractly, and the ubiquitous desire to judge the content by the characteristics of the author's personality and identity.

GQ Magazine has committed all four of these errors in an asinine list put together bashing some classic literature, and suggesting more preferable alternatives to them. Dana Schwartz has also written a rather pitiful defense of this article in Entertainment Weekly which is possibly worse than the original article itself. Now why do I care about what GQ Magazine has to say about books? Well, because I care about books, I care about cultural influence, and GQ has a total circulation of about one million if we're using the 2013 figures. If it can influence men into being unbearable metrosexuals, then it can influence their views on literature I'm sure of it. Both of these pieces I'm going to cover precisely why the

Humanities get mocked nine ways to Sunday in the modern era.

My interests have always rested within the Humanities primarily in the realm of Literature, and I am deeply opposed to the study of Literature and the interpretation of said Literature being a practice in reading through a microscope of your own personal neuroses. There is still much debate in the world of books about the concept of "literary merit" by itself. Those who critique this idea are rightly stating that any field of art critique is necessarily subjective because aesthetic value is purely driven by personal taste. This is largely true, one can judge a piece of literature to be good or bad based on a variety of reasons and have it be legitimate. Perhaps they don't like the way the sentences are structured? Maybe they don't think the characters are well-rounded enough? Is there not enough action in the book?

One notices that all of these grievances are a result of the content of the work absent outside forces. I'm not here to argue that books can be objectively good, and objectively bad. What I am here to argue is that one cannot hide behind the subjective nature of the art world to justify interpretations that do not come from an examination of the work itself, but come from the critic's political opinions imposing themselves on the work. An example of this would be a Soviet remarking that Animal Farm is a piss-poor novel due to its anti-Soviet themes. A legitimate subjective interpretation, surely. However, it should be noticed that the reader in this case is imposing a non-literary criteria on the novelist in order to get a good review. In order to please this particular critic, the writer must write a novel either totally neutral regarding the Soviet cause, or display Soviet sympathies in some fashion. One can see why I related this to a tainting of the mind. This type of brain staining prevents the enjoyment of literature for its own sake, and puts the burden on the author to be entirely agreeable to the reader before he can be said to have written a "good book."

It's judging literature like it's an argumentative thesis as opposed to a story from which ideas about the human condition can be implanted. It's not the quality and accuracy of a description that's being judged, it's what the author is describing, the context surrounding the novel, from what political angle they are describing it, and whether the author has the critic's seal of approval before diving into a work. It's like saying *Fear and Loathing in Las Vegas* is a terrible novel because you're personally opposed to recreational drug consumption. While I cannot say that this is an objectively incorrect method of examining literature I don't think it is too far-fetched to say that this mindset is a negative influence on the reader, critic, and author. We will deal with GQ's article first, then set our sights on Dana Schwartz's attempt at defending it. Much of the article consists of what I imagine are writers doing their best to separate themselves from the masses by having a vague subjective irrefutable contrarian view of certain literary classics. Many of them consist of things like:

*"Catch-22 fails to capture the absurdities and impossible conflicts of war" or "The Old Man and the Sea left me unmoved. Mostly, I kept hoping the fish would get away without too much damage. (When my grandpa pushed me to catch a trout at a fish farm, I threw the rod into the pond)."*

The first one I find to be more to be a case of reader failure as opposed to author failure. The second being an author who finds the act of fishing cruel, had a bad experience fishing once with his grandfather, and so for some reason simply cannot empathize with the disappointment that comes from a figurative lifetime of hard work and optimistic persistence ultimately ending in yet another failure, and the connection that man and the rest of nature have in the concept of death. See what I mean about personal neuroses? These are shallow literalists who are not to be taken seriously when it comes to literature. I get the impression that these facile opinions and half-jokes are nothing more than defense mechanisms for those who didn't understanding the material, but still desperately want to say something clever about it. The story, while being about a man and fish, is not merely about a man and a fish. These types of criticisms come from the worst kinds of readers.

Here is how the GQ article begins:

*"We've been told all our lives that we can only call ourselves well-read once we've read the Great Books. We tried. We got halfway through Infinite Jest and halfway through the SparkNotes on Finnegans Wake. But a few pages into Bleak House, we realized that not all the Great Books have aged well. Some are racist and some are sexist, but most are just really, really boring. So we—and a group of un-boring writers—give you permission to strike these books from the canon. Here's what you should read instead."*

If you can stomach this kind of pomposity, then any smugness I display should pale in comparison. The first critique comes from Lauren Groff, which states:

*"I actually love Lonesome Dove, but I'm convinced that the cowboy mythos, with its rigid masculine emotional landscape, glorification of guns and destruction, and misogynistic gender roles, is a major factor in the degradation of America. Rather than perpetuate this myth, I'd love for everyone, but particularly American men, to read The Mountain Lion by Jean Stafford. It's a wicked, brilliant, dark book set largely on a ranch in Colorado, but it acts in many ways as a strong rebuttal to all the old toxic western stereotypes we all need to explode."*

This is a perfect example of the error in literary critique I mentioned when the reader is too obsessed with contemporary politics. It makes them unable to judge a novel as a novel, and instead treat it like an enemy IED. One wonders whether this critic would recommend this book if she didn't believe that its mythic themes are a major factor in the degradation of America. Remarking that she loves the book, but won't recommend it because of the present political landscape is laughable as a literary critique. She also tacitly admits that she loves something she considers to promote toxic attitudes and behaviors.

The critic places themselves in an odd position when they recommend literature, or don't recommend it, based on political landscape. One argument for objective literary merit is the aspect of timelessness and whether one can relate to the characters in a book regardless of what time and place they happen to be living in. In essence, this critic is not trying to give you decent book recommendations. This critic is trying to get her ideas implanted into the psyche of American men, and so recommends a book based on political expediency. One notices immediately that were it not for her obvious preoccupation with the idea of "toxic masculinity," and her paranoid view of the male sex, she would easily recommend this book to the audience of GQ Magazine. Although there is a hint of fear in her voice which suggests that this book will turn men toxic.

It's not the book she is critiquing here, it's men, and how they allegedly wouldn't be able to handle such poisonous material. I see the mindset of the censorious publisher slowly taking form in her as well. I'm unsure of her attitude on the publishing of toxic material that she thinks is contributing to the degradation of America, but it certainly brings one back to the days of the English publishing industry of the early 20th century. It was defined by a small cabal of literary publishing masterminds who were terrified of publishing any work of fiction containing themes that were critical of the Soviet Union. If I could be so bold, I find this attitude surrounding art and literature to be much more "toxic" and degrading to American society than any novel about cowboys.

The second point that stuck out to me was Omar El Akkad's take on Robert Grave's autobiographical piece "Goodbye to All That" which reads as follows:

*"Goodbye to All That, the autobiographical account of Graves's time in the trenches during World War I, is entertaining and enlightening. It's also incredibly racist. Graves includes samples of near unintelligible essays produced by three of his students ("Mahmoud Mohammed Mahmoud," "Mohammed Mahmoud Mohammed," and "Mahmoud Mahmoud Mohammed") from his postwar stint as an English instructor in Cairo. The joke is twofold—all these silly natives have similar-sounding names, and they lack the basic intellectual capacity to grapple with the literature. A better option is Dispatches by Michael Herr. It concerns a different time, country, and war, but this is still, in my mind, the most indispensable personal account of the cruelty and violence of modern warfare."*

Omar El Akkad is an Egyptian-Canadian novelist and journalist, and one can't help but think that he is apprehensive to

Graves' portrayal of his Egyptian English students performing poorly and having similar names partly due to his Egyptian heritage. This scene occurs in Chapter 32 of the book and is presented right before Graves decides to resign from his position. Graves is giving his reasoning for abandoning his position as examiner of a diploma class of Literature students. One expects these kinds of admissions in an autobiography. The essays given were indeed unintelligible, the second of which not being an essay at all, only containing a few plagiarized quotes from Shakespeare. If he was having difficulty teaching students to such a degree I'm not surprised that Graves decided to quit.

The interpretation that Graves was being racist is practically a non-interpretation in my view, or stems from a misreading of the material entirely. Graves describes the failure of the students in the context of European colonialism (one remembers the November 1914 British protectorate) coupled with the volatile state of Egyptian politics, not by the fact that they are Egyptian and on that basis, inferior as human beings. I doubt that Omar El Akkad read this work cover to cover, or if he did he's having manufactured memories of experiencing racism from Robert Graves. Eventually we must recognize as a society that while interpretation is subjective, making snide suggestions that an author is a bigot does not fall within subjective interpretation. If Robert Graves was feeling a tad down in the dumps about the failure of his Egyptian students I can say with certainty that I'm experiencing a similar feeling when it comes to a certain Egyptian-Canadian novelist.

Keeping on in the same vein is the claim further down in the article that Mark Twain was a racist is, for one, not literary critique, and two an outright fabrication concerning one of the 1800s most noteworthy polemicists. Mark Twain wrote argumentative essays in his later years against anti-Semitism, an essay opposing the culture of lynching, a denunciation of imperialism, and a pamphlet savagely critiquing the Belgian's cruel rule in the Congo. He donated all of the proceeds from that pamphlet to the victims of King Leopold's rule as well. To say that Mark Twain was a racist is to put too much stock into the uttering of racial slurs in his novels, and on rare occasion in letters.

*The Adventures of Huckleberry Finn* is about a kid trying to assist a runaway slave, and at one point in the novel lying to search parties about Jim's race when interrogated. This is not the work of an author who has a contaminated moral compass when it comes to race relations. If you'd like to check out these essays for yourself they are titled in the order I've mentioned them:

1. Concerning the Jews
2. The United States of Lyncherdom
3. To The Man Sitting In Darkness
4. King Leopold's Soliloquy

Trying to spread the narrative that Mark Twain was a racist is a disservice and a shameful display in this article. Imagine living in the mid to late 1800s, writing scathing critiques of imperialism and various forms of racism, and then around 150 years later having the literary minds of that time calling you a racist, or the horrifically euphemistic phrase: "A man of his time."

The final portion of this article I would like to deal with is with Nadja Spiegelman's reason for why she thinks Slaughterhouse Five by Kurt Vonnegut deserves a spot on this list.

*"When men on dating apps list a book, they invariably list Slaughterhouse-Five. I'd rather not get a drink with a person who's taking his cues from Vonnegut: The few women in Slaughterhouse-Five die early, are porn stars, or are "bitchy flibbertigibbets."*

Another glib attacking of men who say they like *Slaughterhouse-Five* in dating apps. It's no wonder she's single. I can assure her that men who like *Slaughterhouse-Five* are completely uninterested in getting a drink with her, especially if she's so myopic as to think enjoying a novel by Kurt Vonnegut is something of a character defect. This precedes a complaint that she doesn't like how the author handles female characters. I think I can give an arguably surrealist book about war and the Dresden bombing featuring genderless time-traveling aliens, and wrestling with the "war means manly glory" concept told through an unreliable narrator a pass on having a prominent female cast. I suppose what irked me the most about this article is not the recommendations themselves, but in the idea that these classics should be replaced by alternatives because they are too racist, too boring, too traditionally manly, not traditionally female enough, or not sensitive enough to the reader's particular paranoia, or political proclivities.

Onward though comes a defense by Dana Schwartz who uses a few dubious methods to defend this absolutely pitiful display of an article. I'll be going over her main defenses here, not fisking the entirety of her article.

The first is an accusation that those opposed to this article are guilty of "pearl-clutching." That those who expressed distaste for this article are simply being outraged online, and have been successfully trolled by the Editors of GQ Magazine. While I'm all for a good bit of trolling I never expected GQ, an alleged men's magazine, to write articles purely to see the upset reaction on the part of their readership. I've sure been had. If only I were aware that GQ was so dedicated to trolling me that they would officially publish nonsensical garbage in their magazine just to pull the wool over my eyes. I don't think the remark about Mark Twain being a racist was just a fine bit of trolling. It was a serious statement. If this is the case then I could practically say anything and decide that it was just to make my audience mad if they disagree with me. Could it not be said that some of these critics were engaging in pearl-clutchery as well since one decided that *The Old Man and The Sea* was bad because he had a bad experience fishing once. Disagreeing with the dismissal of classic literature based on nothing but narcissism and personal discomfort is the opposite of pearl-clutching. It is the opposition to pearl-clutching. No one should be told that disagreement is pearl-clutching, and thus, criticizing the act of literary pearl-clutching is by definition an act of hypocrisy. It isn't.

Schwartz's second defense attempt states:

*"GQ isn't actually telling you not to read these books; several of the*

*contributing authors actually admit to loving the books they're suppos-*
*edly maligning. Instead, the purpose of the article is to liberate you*
*from the idea that you have to read these books, that reading them*
*cover to cover and checking them off some invisible list is essential to*
*your very existence and if you don't you'll never be able to show your*
*face in Brooklyn again."*

I appreciate Dana's unwavering grasp of the obvious, but I
doubt anyone critiquing this article genuinely thought they
were under the jurisdiction of GQs reading list. The article
was not merely an attempt to liberate us from the idea that we
have to read these books and a rebuke of a cultural literary
hegemony. There were multiple factually inaccurate statements in the article, plus the reasoning for dismissing these
works consisted of the critics expressing how uncomfortable it
made them. The self-centeredness of the critiques is what set
people off, not the fact that they GQ controls what books
they are allowed to read. Some of the authors do admit to
loving the books, but this doesn't stop them from advocating
they be replaced by "woker" counterparts. Schwartz then
attempts to bring everybody together by saying that it's a good
thing that everyone disagrees about the merit of various
classics.

*"Anyone who purports to loving literature should be grateful that*
*books, like all art, elicit new and distinct responses in its audiences and*
*that taste is not monolithic. It's a good thing some people love Catch-22*
*and some people think, like New York Times reviewer Roger H. Smith*
*did at the time, "its author cannot write." Cool! Art is fun because we*
*all feel differently about it! It prompts discussions and disagreements*
*and interpretations. Staunchly fetishizing certain books as unimpeach-*
*able, as above critique or conversation, is contrary to the purpose of art*
*in the first place."*

I mean, apart from the disingenuous pearl-clutching that
she just accused us of having of course. Schwartz conflates
people taking issue with the specific criticisms of classic works
leveled by the article, and the idea that these works are above
criticism. For example, I love *A Farewell To Arms*, but if
someone were to tell me that they hate it due to Hemingway's
writing style. I would get it. In fact, this happens within the

GQ article, and it should be noted that I did not criticize that particular point. She then re-emerges from her cross-legged posture and "kumbaya" mantra to say this towards the end of the article:

*"In truth, the GQ article is a gift to readers: it provides new recommendations for books you may not have been exposed to in high school. Clickbait-y headline aside (and remember, we all need to make a living), the purpose of the article is just to show that the literary world is broader and more interesting than the titles that you've seen on "best of" lists again and again, those endless, tiresome lists that cannibalize and sustain each other like a oroborus of middle-grade prestige fiction. Bringing attention to books that are less male, and less white, is not a bad thing after centuries of culture that reinforced that white male stories were the only ones which mattered."*

There's the kicker. It's not about the literature. It's not about the story. It's not about the themes and motifs, the plots, the beauty of language, or the moral lessons that can be taken from literature. It's the personification of novels forcing them to take on the identity of the author. We've already heard every "white" story before. We've already heard every "male" story before, right? The white male is a boring cliché to these people, and while they think they are broadening the horizons of readers the truth is they are advocating its restriction. The age of the "White Male" author has come and gone. Their existence is a cliché. It's time to let the new, exotic, and "fresh" authors take the wheel. Everyone totally knows by now that the *Sherlock Holmes* series by Sir Arthur Conan Doyle, *Crime and Punishment* by Fyodor Dostoyevsky, and Stephen King's *It* are all essentially the same story. If you've read one "White Male" you've read them all, right?

# ORDER AND CHAOS AT THE
# THEATER

There I was, a wannabe freelance journalist hoping to cover an event that I didn't even have a ticket to. I hadn't been aware that Jordan Peterson was going to be in the Boston area until the theater had sold out. Clearly he's been doing well for himself with his rocketing into stardom around two years ago, and since I'm right in his golden demographic (a young millennial man) I thought I'd take a listen to what some of his supporters and fans have to say about him. It wouldn't be a comprehensive report, unless my contact came through for me of course, and since I hadn't heard from them all day it seemed like the whole thing was doomed to miserable failure.

I took the easy way out and ordered an Uber out to a dive bar near the theater, accompanied on the road for a long while by a fellow Uber customer. I could tell it was one of those ride-sharing app situations almost immediately because the driver was a young and slightly disheveled looking teenager while the passenger was a man in a suit screaming at someone else over the phone. Maybe a business deal gone bad? Got fired? An emergency completely unrelated to work? I had no idea. I spoke with the driver a bit about the differences between Boston and New York City, it eventually turned into a friendly round of banter about which city is better than the other. In the interest of fairness I conceded the point to the driver about how New York City's streets are far easier to navigate, and I can imagine that's important to someone in the driving profession.

We parted ways and I made my way towards the door of the bar. The door was closed which is a bit odd for a bar in Boston, generally during the spring and summertime they leave the front doors open in the afternoons, only bringing the bouncers around after the sun goes down. As I walk in I'm greeted with a few booths on the left, and the standard Church Choir of liquor bottles behind the counter on the right. There were only around five or six customers there when I arrived, they were all talking to the staff as if they knew them, and I realized quite quickly that I was the only person there who wasn't a regular. The walls of the place were decorated with replicas of signed instruments, pictures, cymbals, and old firearms. It screamed 70s dive bar and I think that's what they were going for. There was a small hole in the brick wall behind the booths just deep enough to seem like the result of a construction accident, but just shallow and exact enough that it could be intended as decoration.

I sent out a Tweet asking anyone in the area to meet me at this bar for some pre-event discussion so I could pick their brains a bit, but I wasn't expecting anyone to show up and no one did. I decided to order a beer because my scrambled attempt at grabbing a story had been hopelessly squandered by my own incompetence and lack of access. So I decided to get settled into one of those precious "drinking alone in a dive bar on a Monday" kinds of evenings.

For someone who hadn't read Jordan Peterson's most recent book, the title claiming that he has the antidote to chaos, I was in precisely the wrong spot. All of the music playing in the background boasted of a tumultuous life and so did the interior design. A picture of a topless woman hovered over the men and women ordering drinks. It looked like a bar that biker gangs, depressed salesmen in loosened ties, downtrodden unpublished writers, or sheltered college kids looking to get some cheap kicks would hang out in. I was the only one who fit any of those descriptions present though, the only young people in this place consisted of the staff and myself. I suppose a place like this is perfect for old-timers to reminisce about the glory days, and remark about how things aren't quite as good as they used to be.

I've always had the skill of eavesdropping mainly due to how average and ineffectual I look. Nobody thinks some scrawny kid in a plain t-shirt, glasses, jeans, and a pair of beaten up brown dress shoes is going to do anything worth paying attention to.

Two older men began discussing how they were in college when Bob Dylan was an up and coming musical sensation, and how Yoko Ono single-handedly drove the Beatles into the dirt. One of them was more clearly stuck in a past decade than the other, telling a tale about how his mother found some illegal drugs in his dresser when he was a teenager. After this story of juvenile mischief though, the guy began pounding vodka sodas with lime like someone stranded in the desert discovering an oasis of fresh water. He ordered one after he finished the first. Then another. Then another. Then another requesting a fresh glass this time all in the span of about thirty minutes.

"Jesus Christ," I thought "Well, he's pretty hefty and he probably knows where his limit is."

⚜

AROUND 6:00PM, AN HOUR AND A HALF BEFORE SHOW TIME, a couple of suited men who had to have been in their early or mid-forties came walking in. Both engineers as I recall. One ordered a white wine; the other ordered a Miller Lite and busted the wine drinker's balls over his drink of choice. Ordering wine in a bar like this would be like asking for a side of caviar at a burger joint. Eventually the wine drinker's friend pressured him into buying a beer to "wash that wine down with."

The bald chubby guy who practically guzzled his mixed drinks began trying to have a drunken conversation with the engineers, trying to give them fun facts about different decorations on the walls. He tried to buy everyone drinks, but I

45

refused out of kindness. One of my rules of life is, never accept the offer to have a drink bought for you by someone who is already plastered; it's entirely possible and usually quite likely that they won't have enough to pay for it. Then you're stuck with a bill that you might not be able to afford all because some guy in a bar got too drunk to remember that his bank account balance only had one zero on the end as opposed to two. Plus he may have already blacked out and I wouldn't want him to wake up the next morning wondering how in the world he drank that much last night when he didn't.

He tried to anchor himself to the Earth by repeating "I see nothing I know nothing" famously said by Sergeant Schultz from Hogan's Heroes. The alcohol was bringing his insecurities forward and he began to compliment the other older gentlemen on their full heads of hair. I couldn't be too hard on the guy. He just desperately wanted someone to talk to, and for that someone to find him a bit interesting. This has to be a form of mild Chaos according to the definitions Peterson uses.

There are varying interpretations of Peterson's work much like there are varying interpretations of religious texts. Most likely because of all of the metaphorical language, and the difficulty in grasping what is trying to be expressed that results from its overuse. I didn't necessarily want an antidote to Chaos, because Chaos is where all of my stories came from. When I broke a rule, strayed off the well-trodden path, defied convention, did something bold, or got into a fight. Nobody tells exciting stories to their grandchildren about the time they finally got that promotion from middle management to upper management. Maybe they do. Maybe others find stories like that exciting. I couldn't drum up any definitive opinion about the book itself because I hadn't read it, and the preview you're given on Amazon Books was most likely missing context I would need. Although it did speak of finding a balance between order and chaos which was slightly odd for a book allegedly delivering one of its antidotes.

Did Peterson have a solution for someone whose life needed an antidote to Order? While we do see people's lives inadvertently fall into Chaos if they aren't attentive enough, we also see people's lives inadvertently fall into Order. Just as someone can get lazy at their job and get fired, someone can zone out and then awaken from autopilot ten years later wondering where all the time went and wishing they had done more exciting and dare I say "Chaotic" things when they were in their twenties. It is very possible that some people need Chaos to find meaning that they are happy with. What is a mid-life crisis after all if not someone whose life has had too much Order in the early stages, and so they introduce some Chaos in the middle of it to shake things up a bit?

I think I get what he's trying to do though. He's trying to get your innate psychology to work for you instead of against you. The reason he uses mythological stories so often is because he's looking for consistent themes or undercurrents in the psychologies of cultures across centuries to find some basic foundation to build his method off of, in an attempt to prove "moral truths." But this leaves Peterson's efforts in the hands of the writers, the myth-tellers, the orators, and the artists. All of us know just how psychologically compromised many artists can be. I wouldn't want any psychologist leafing through "Lolita" centuries from now wondering why we thought Humbert was the perfect example of a human being. But then again, our culture didn't exactly worship this character like others did various manifestations of God and his Messiah. If we're using that metric though, mass worship, then there must be some kind of biological psychological case to be made for why Muhammad is someone a large portion of the human population thinks is a "perfect example of a human being." What makes one religion an example of useful moral truth, and another a harmful moral lie? By what metric are we measuring this? Anyway, I'm getting ahead of myself.

I knew if I didn't read every single line of Peterson's work before commenting on it his more diehard enthusiasts would zero in on precisely which line I'd missed, how it explained what I got wrong, and how stupid I was for not grasping something so trivially obvious. Wouldn't want to dig that grave for myself obviously. I didn't have time to read it now. I'd been too focused on other things recently, and the book is a little bit pricey for someone in my income bracket. Peterson's lecture should give me a decent enough clear synopsis of the book to draw something meaningful from. I've never been one for self-help, but he seems to be connecting with people for one reason or another, so I might as well subject myself to what his audience sees in him.

I ORDERED A WHISKEY NEAT AND IT WAS PUT DOWN ON THE table right as I was getting a phone call. It was the person who offered to get me into the theater asking if I was still interested! The night might not be ruined after all. They told me to talk to any of the ticket scanners and ask to see the manager then they would sort me out. There was around an hour before show time and I'd finished a beer on an empty stomach, and now had a whiskey to deal with in front of me. I grabbed some quick and cheap food from the bar to keep the whiskey at bay and headed to the theater.

On the way there a man in a dirty sweatshirt was holding a thin cardboard sign that read: "My Life Sucks. I Need Money." I gave him seventy-five cents, and then crossed the street.

Unfortunately, I scarfed the food and whiskey down quicker than anticipated. No one was in line yet, and they weren't letting anyone through. So I stopped at a restaurant directly next door and hung around their bar for a little while. It was a higher class place, showing off that they had a cook that was on Hell's Kitchen with signs in front to draw folks in. Lots of people were grouped up in here waiting for the show to begin. The place was packed, but not so much that I couldn't squeeze my way to the counter.

I was expecting to see a large throng of young men waiting to get in to see Jordan Peterson, but I was surprised to see people of both sexes and a diverse age range among them. I even saw families with young children wandering around outside patiently waiting for the lecture to begin. I listened in on the conversations, and whenever someone who wasn't there to see the show asked what everyone was waiting for the answers were largely the same.

"Well he's like a self-help psychologist guy and he talks about like getting your act together and stuff." I mean, they aren't wrong. This shiny prism-covered place is where the business-men get drunk and rowdy, get kicked out, and then stumble over the block to the bar I'd just returned from. I stayed here until 7:15 and then rushed out to try and get a decent place in line. It took me around five minutes to get from the back of the line to the front. Right inside the front doors there was a huge bearded man scanning the crowd with what I could only assume was a drug-sniffing dog at his side. The poor thing was a very old Labrador Retriever and his eyes told me everything. The last place that pitiful puppy wanted to be was running his nose across a bunch of half-drunks hoping to get their life in order. He looked up at me like he was begging for a treat, but his eyebrows said "Get me out of here."

I'd finally reached the front of the line. I asked to see the manager and they asked me my name. I gave it to them and they brought me over to a side table. I was handed a ticket for an unused seat and just like that I was in. It was at this point I realized I went from the architectural, social, and musical manifestation of Chaos to the very definition of Order too quickly. Every job title here had its own uniform, people were filing in like they were on a conveyor belt, and the only chaotic element introduced in this scenario was alcohol being served. Everything else was clean, dusted, and proper. I suppose it had to be since very fancy philharmonics played here. On the other hand, so have The Wiggles.

Rushing to the door to try and sit down before the fanfare started I was stopped by someone checking tickets a second time. A wave of anxiety flowed through my body, but it turns out he was just trying to help me find my seat. An employee followed me all the way down to my row and watched as I sat down. A kind gesture in their minds I'm sure. How intoxicated do people usually get here that they need someone assisting them with the English Alphabet? It must just be another perk of the "high class theater" experience.

The announcer's booming voice quaked over the PA system reiterating the usual "turn off your cellphone out of respect for the other audience members" generic paragraph. But in addition to this it was stated powerfully that the theater has a "zero tolerance policy" for heckling which was met with thunderous applause from the audience. To my surprise Dave Rubin was opening for Peterson trying to get the crowd warmed up. Every reference to lobsters was met with hearty chuckles from the crowd. Rubin also remarked about how incredible the Intellectual Dark Web Phenomenon is with Sam Harris on the left and Ben Shapiro on the right having these wonderful debates and discussions and all of that jazz.

I was able to get around forty seconds of footage before the staff rushed over and told me to put the camera away. Expected. They don't want people to be able to see the event without paying something first. Ruins the air of edgy secrecy the "Intellectual Dark Web" name puts out too. I put the camera away and the staff member moseyed on back to wherever their "phone camera watch post" was.

Peterson was met with a standing ovation. He announced that he was writing the introduction to the anniversary edition of the Gulag Archipelago, and that was also met with roaring cheers.

I WENT TO PETERSON'S LECTURE TO GET A SYNOPSIS OF HIS self-help book, but left slightly disappointed. There were several tangents about how the Marxists got it wrong, how the post-modernists got it wrong, how the Universities are to blame for a lot of the collectivist attitudes we are seeing recently, a few symbolic metaphorical build-ups, a couple of personal stories, and a praising of the West in regards to the sovereignty of the individual. During the entire hour and a half long talk he only mentioned one of the rules in the book! It could be boiled down to "stand tall and be reasonably confident when taking on the world." I could've heard different versions of his advice by skimming Meditations by Marcus Aurelius or watching the Rocky movies. The language is much simpler too. One doesn't need to be well-versed in psychology, mythology, anthropology, sociology, and philosophy to grasp it either.

I didn't feel helped so much as I felt like I knew a few more rebuttals against Marxists and post-modernist thinkers, and was thrown into something of an existential crisis when he tried to explain value structures and dominance hierarchies. I remember being off-put by the idea of self-help that has a political message built into it. It reminded me of the revulsion I still feel at Alcoholics Anonymous telling everyone that they have to turn to Jesus in order to fix their addiction. Whenever I'm dealing with someone in the self-help field my guard is up due to their propensity to prey on the vulnerable.

I started getting flashbacks to when I accidentally sat through an advanced college course as a freshman, and the internally focused embarrassment pushed itself to the fore-front of my mind. I was unable to distinguish between gibber-ish, profundity, and platitude as if I'd been given some supplementary material to read and shirked this responsibility, which I had, considering I hadn't purchased the book yet. Was I far too stupid to understand him here, or was he just rambling? I couldn't tell.

Whenever one is dealing with Peterson it's like opening up a brand new edition of the English language where "religion" can be defined as "any axiomatic belief," and where "metaphys-ical truth" replaces "the suspension of disbelief" and "moral lessons" when it comes to story-telling. How does one judge which moral lessons are metaphysical truth and which are metaphysical lies? Is there some kind of objective method of doing so? What makes Christian symbolism an example of metaphysical truth that can't also be applied to the Islamic faith? Can one determine metaphysical truth from metaphys-ical lie without referencing the physical? If they can't wouldn't that make whatever statement is being examined another example of empirical truth or empirical lie? This wasn't in the same zip code as my pay-grade, and so I put the questions out of my mind.

Before this point I thought I was living a pretty okay life for someone whose only skill was with words, but I guess there are abstract metaphorical concepts beyond my mind's comprehension that I either needed to spend more time thinking about or fly away from forever. Being something of a ruminator these questions would only further my innate mental turmoil. It was difficult to understand him, but then again, he makes himself very difficult to understand. I have to imagine that many of the people who claim they "get him" the first time around are lying up a storm, or perhaps I have a comprehension problem. For most of his time on stage it didn't seem like he was trying to outline his book so much as he was having a constant debate with himself, pacing across the stage, and talking with his hands.

I filed out of the theater with a couple of nice people who recognized me and we had a nice chat about Peterson's material. I couldn't contribute much to the conversation due to my ignorance, but I listened intently. One of them remarked that Peterson had changed the way he looked at the world and it affected him in a very positive way. He told me a personal story that I won't detail here that made me understand why some find immense value in Peterson's words. All I can do is take him at his word there.

Maybe every generation needs a public figure to channel old classic wisdom through. Ultimately though, in this humble author's opinion, there will never be a final spark of clarity. There will never be a moment of full enlightenment. An infallible system will never exist. There will never be a universal path to happiness, meaning, and fulfillment. We will always be internally struggling and trying to force ourselves out of contradictions by tweaking an idea here and adjusting a thought there. No one ever gets better at this activity. The more intelligent one gets the better at rationalizing to oneself one gets. It's an eternal fight that all of us must endure once we reach the age of reason. It never gets easier. The trick is to try and have fun with it.

# THE HANDMAID'S TALE: A
# SUCCESSFUL FLOP

Anyone looking to denigrate a dystopian story can fall back on accusing the author of being pretentious and paranoid. If the work is meant to be speculative or literary in any capacity then it's practically built upon a solid base of self-importance. On some minute level the writer believes that the world they've created is possible and the book is meant to be a harrowing look into a potential future should we blindly continue along our current path. The author believes themselves to have a type of foresight that the general population lacks. This can be part of the charm if it is leveraged in the right ways. Condemning a dystopian novel writer over excessive conde- scension is much like telling someone who wrote a biography that they are an obsessive stalker, but hear me out.

Margaret Atwood's novel *The Handmaid's Tale* is the perfect example of a book that did not get by on its merits, but by the alleged "warning it delivers," the "impact it has," and the "mes- sage it sends." Dystopian novels are nearly always interpreted incorrectly by activists in order to push a cause of some type. They enlist the author into a fight that they might not want to participate in without their consent. On occasion doing so posthumously. Whenever this work of hers is mentioned posi- tively in common conversation it's almost always because of how "true it is," or how much, "closer we are to Atwood's prediction."

I don't think I'm going too far to say that this is a form of mass delusion, mass ignorance, or mass inauthenticity. Most of her admirers are able to overlook a colander-like plot, characters that resemble mannequins in their depth, and unnecessary tangents about the mundane in order to shower praise upon mediocrity.

To give a short summary, the world the characters live in has been turned into an oppressive patriarchal totalitarian regime based on a fundamentalist reading of the Old Testament. Women and men are both under the boot-heel of a religiously motivated caste system, and due to a massive rise in infertility, fertile women are assigned to an upper crust couple to act as a surrogate. Their freedom is essentially evacuated and they are forced into being the property of the man they are hoping to conceive a child for. If Offred (the main character) cannot get pregnant after two years' time she is then cast out as an "Unwoman," made to live in grotesque conditions, and perform almost certainly fatal hard labor.

In April of 2017, the New Yorker crowned Atwood the "prophet of dystopia," doing all but starting a religion in her Messianic name. Atwood refused this title officially when she was made aware of it, but then gave the mantle a sensual wink and come-hither gaze by remarking about how she is, "sorry to have been so right." The totalitarian regime of Gilead was implemented when a radical fundamentalist Christian group known as the "Son of Jacob" conducted an attack on the U.S government which killed the President. They also mowed down Congress with machine guns, blamed the attack on Islamic radicals, and suspended the Constitution.

I would love to dive further into just how this group organized the attack, how they were able to bypass the Secret Service, how they were able to suspend the Constitution without much pushback from the American Army, why the Army seemed to be completely willing to enforce the new laws, and why the American People were so willing to accept that their wives, daughters, and mothers were now classed as property. Unfortunately, I can't do that because Atwood gives nary much more than my explanation here. For a book that is supposed to be "speculative fiction" concerned about power dynamics it was surprising that Atwood seems to hand wave away the most powerful physical force within the U.S government, The Army, and portray the men and women serving as an amorphous mass of brutes who only exist to serve the whims of anyone that decides to claim power. Being the master of dystopia, power dynamics and speculative fiction that she is, Atwood deals with the suspension of the Constitution and the complexities of that sudden dramatic change in one boring uneventful sentence:

*"That was when they suspended the Constitution."*

Atwood wastes the time that could be spent expanding on the important details of this "timeless warning," by forcing her protagonist to consistently whine about her appearance, ramble about trivialities, and preoccupy herself with self-obsessed sexual and romantic urges. Much of the time I forgot that I was supposed to be reading a literary dystopian classic and began to wonder why I was browsing through a completely forgettable romantic thriller.

The reader understands that there must be a certain level of disbelief suspension when browsing fiction, but Atwood uses this as an excuse for simple unsatisfying explanations and insults us with her low expectations. It is revealed at the end of the novel that the story of Offred was discovered on tape recordings in an army surplus store in Maine. Certainly an interesting concept, but browsing back through the novel after this revelation, it doesn't excuse the useless stream-of-consciousness style that Atwood employs. The main character behaves as if she is completely brainwashed by the Gilead system, at some points being unable to remember the past, yet the regime has only been in power for three years.

I started to recall Winston Smith and his struggle to put together some objective view of the past in light of Big Brother utterly erasing and altering historical fact. Atwood appears to selectively slap this uncertainty on her main character as well when she wants to give off the illusion of depth despite eschewing the ever so droll idea that she has to explain why the character simultaneously can and can't remember the state of the world from less than five years ago. Atwood also uses the terms "Unwoman" and "Unbaby" to describe women that are sentenced to exile and hard labor, and infants that are born misshapen or diseased. This is a direct lifting of the phrase "Unperson" present in the state of Oceania. She borrows the caste system concept from Huxley, complete with different colored uniforms for women depending on their role in society. Red for the Handmaids, blue for the Wives, green for the Marthas, etc etc.

There are also passages where our main character is speaking in the present tense presumably into the recorder when it would have been impossible, impractical, or dangerous in the moment. The protagonist doesn't have nearly an interesting enough voice to pull off a literary found footage documentary either. Whenever I started to become mildly captivated by the juvenile ramblings of the main character, Margaret Atwood would chime in with a long clumsy simile snatching me by the collar and pulling me out of the story for no other purpose aside from reminding me that she is there:

*"Night falls. Or has fallen. Why is it that night falls, instead of rising, like the dawn? Yet if you look east, at sunset, you can see night rising, not falling; darkness lifting into the sky, up from the horizon, like a black sun behind cloud cover. Like smoke from an unseen fire, a line of fire just below the horizon, brushfire or a burning city. Maybe night falls because it's heavy, a thick curtain pulled up over the eyes. Wool blanket. I wish I could see in the dark, better than I do."*

The propaganda oozing out of the Republic of Gilead is so powerful that it renders Offred's memory unreliable after a few years' time, but despite the fact that she is not allowed to read she can still speak in terribly pretentious purple prose. While inconsistency is the bedrock of totalitarian regimes, inconsistencies such as these are not cute, clever, intentional, or symbolic. They are the products of lazy writing being shoehorned into literary prominence. I recall audibly laughing when I discovered that a secret passage helping women escape the Gilead regime was named, "The Underground

Femaleroad." One might as well name the leader of the resistance Martha Luther King Jr. at that point.

Atwood's writing improves during sex scenes, and the intense moments toward the end. Credit where credit is due, I've read no one who describes passionless and mechanical sex quite as beautifully. When one imagines, "sex solely for the purposes of procreation," one has to take the "solely" bit seriously. Being the one of the most intimate activities undertaken by our species it is difficult for one to divorce the ideas of physical pleasure and emotional fulfillment from the act. A ceremony where the "Commander" Offred is assigned to attempts to inseminate her while she clutches the hands of his wife, Serena Joy, is possibly the most unsettling and uncomfortable portrayal of sex outside of Marquis-style vulgarity.

Despite how much I dislike "as a..." statements, as a man who was raised in what would be called a "traditionally masculine" way, one of the most interesting scenes in the novel is when the main character's internal monologue is reveling in the sexual power she has over men of low status. Deemed unworthy for reproduction, too young to be responsible for the situation these characters find themselves in, and yet she still rolls her hips in front of sexually repressed men who know they don't have a chance at any form of physical intimacy. There's no reason to do this aside from transferring the suffering to another person.

The main character has had her freedom evacuated, and as such, finds sick pleasure in reminding the dregs that they'll never have the opportunity to court her. It is one of the very few illuminating glimpses into the realm of power dynamics between the sexes that Atwood provides. Scenes wherein sex and seduction are mentioned are bereft of ornate language concerning the subjects. Powerful and visceral words are used. Some critics of this book malign this use of language as nothing more than cheap shock jocking, but under a system that officially views sex as a dirty shameful necessary thing, it is expected that such harsh language would be used whenever that subject is referenced.

None of these scenes are great enough to unshackle the

book from the weight of its insistence on sacrificing nearly every form of subtlety to ensure that the reader derives the correct "lessons" from the text.

What are the overarching lessons of this cautionary tale? What present behaviors and political influences should I be on the lookout for to avoid this bleak future? Should I become more environmentalist to avoid the novel's declining birthrate due to humanity's inability to preserve the health of the planet? Should I begin advocating against the use of digital currency for the fear that a government could take advantage of this convenience and manipulate it for their own nefarious ends? Should we all be more adamant in the fight to maintain women's rights? All of these suggestions are forced down the throat of the reader. There is no way one can miss them. There's a distinct feeling of disconnect between the causes and results.

Atwood lays some of the responsibility for Gilead on a kind of unthinking militant feminism when the protagonist recounts her mother's activist marches and how they lead to a large scale right-wing backlash. It would've been nice for this concept to take root in the novel and grow as the pages turned, but as is traditional with "The Handmaid's Tale," it tapered off and we don't get much in the form of detail. There are a few short references to rebels somewhere doing something, and a sectarian war going on in the background that's just happening. This world isn't so much an original invention based off of carefully examined projections of where America might be headed. It is a scrambled mish-mosh of dumbed down historical references, a shallow interpretation of American politics, and a poorly mixed gumbo of more insightful dystopian writers. It's seasoned with the ideology of gender-based warfare, then packaged and sold to paranoiacs who have nothing else to worry about aside from their belief that men "only want one thing," and conservatives making monotonous speeches about "returning to traditional family values."

This work is often promoted as "the feminist dystopia," and what an appropriate claim to fame it is. I dread the day when art just becomes another form of ideological warfare with everyone waving their favorite dystopia in the air screeching "The End is nigh" into megaphones. Socialists patrolling the streets with copies of "Germinal" holstered in their belts. Libertarian Capitalists beating people over the head with copies of *Atlas Shrugged*. Those promoting strict laws against drug use utilizing *Brave New World* as a rhetorical flourish. Thanks to the Hulu television series based on *The Handmaid's Tale*, a new edition of book spine truncheon has made its way forward in common parlance.

The novel is praised for its "message," for its "importance in this day and age," for the "impact it has had," for the "warnings it sends," for its "stark glimpse of a future that is all too close to reality." What was it that Mark Twain said? A classic is a book that everybody wants to have read and nobody wants to read? Calling *The Handmaid's Tale*, a classic is appropriate under the Twain definition but completely inappropriate under any commonly used definition. The fact that Atwood has been classed alongside such luminaries as Orwell, Huxley, Arendt, and Bradbury is an insult to the very concept of literature and the intense study of totalitarianism throughout the early to mid-1900s.

The novel is clearly trying to inspire people to become more strident and aggressive in their defense of women's rights to avoid this dreary future, and the reactions to its renewed popularity prove this to be the case. Yet in the novel itself, it is precisely this strident militant feminism that assists in stoking a reactionary revolution. The fundamental issue with dystopian novels is the pandering to dim activists with delusional fears, or perhaps more apt, dim activists co-opting the novel in order to spread delusional fear. It strengthens the resolve of certain activists and guarantees that they will promote it as a pseudo-religious text for years on end, making poor half-witted references to it with every future political development. One must already believe in much of what Atwood believes in order to find the book compelling, prophetic, and a decent metaphor for today's world. Nothing convincing is ever given to the rest of us. The blurb on the book jacket reads as follows:

"*In condensed but eloquent prose, by turns cool-eyed, tender, despairing, passionate, and wry, she reveals to us the dark corners behind the establishment's calm façade, as certain tendencies now in existence are carried to their logical conclusions.*"

I could not disagree more.

# LICENSE TO OFFEND

Ethan Allen was a soldier and a politician who fought in the Revolutionary War. He was a key player in the liberation of Fort Ticonderoga from the British forces. After peace was concluded, Mr. Allen headed to London in order to assist our newly formed country in doing its business with the king. While he was there he heard sneer after sneer about how rude, crass, and simple-minded Americans were. Eventually, he was invited to the townhouse of a great English Lord.

They ate dinner and drank together, but as it happens, Mr. Allen needed to withdraw to the bathroom. He discovered upon entering the bathroom that the only decoration therein was a portrait of George Washington. When Mr. Allen returned to the drawing room, his hosts began to get fidgety because he hadn't mentioned Washington's portrait. The camel's back was finally broken and his host had to ask whether he'd seen the portrait, and Mr. Allen said that he had. They asked if he thought that portrait was appropriately located in the townhouse, and Mr. Allen replied that it was.

His host was astonished at the response and said, "My goodness, appropriate? Washington's portrait in a bathroom?"

Ethan Allen replied, "Yes, where it will do good service. The whole world knows nothing makes an Englishman shit quicker than the sight of George Washington."

That story was recited by Daniel Day Lewis in the role of Abraham Lincoln in a remarkable movie revolving around his Presidency and the passing of the 13<sup>th</sup> Amendment. Do you think that some people would be offended by that story? People who grimace at the use of profanity or a few patriotic Englishmen perhaps? I think the legal case for freedom of speech containing the license to offend is relatively open and shut with the existence of the 1<sup>st</sup> Amendment.

Yes, the 1<sup>st</sup> Amendment includes the right to say offensive and hateful things. Let's try to break down what "being offended" actually is so we have a foundation upon which to have this argument. Being offended is, at its very core, being made uncomfortable by something someone else has said. Why have we decided, as a society, to give this minor negative emotion so much credence?

I think that a perspective delivery is in order. Please take a moment to reflect on your station in comparison to the billions of other people on the planet. You are one person, with your own set of emotions, passions, goals, and sensitive issues. There are billions of other people who have different emotions, passions, goals, and sensitive issues. How arrogant must it be for one of these billions of people to declare an issue, an opinion on an issue, a word, or even a joke off-limits because they have personally taken offense to it? To think that any of us have some emotionally-granted privileged position on our planet that grants us the power to demand billions of people shut their mouths because we find what was said distasteful is to willfully dwell within a solipsistic delusion.

If it is going to be argued that we should shut down speech that offends us, then what authority grants anyone else a more powerful type of offense in relation to my own? It "offends" me when people suggest that I should not be allowed to say something, hear something, or write something because it makes them feel uncomfortable. For some reason, my offense can be tossed aside. Some in this twisted world have decided that they are the arbiters for what is and isn't objectively offensive, and thus, have decided to take matters into their own hands.

We've seen various attempts to shut down speakers in Universities throughout the Western World in the past decade. The three examples that immediately spring to mind for me is when students at the University of Toronto pulled the fire alarm in a bid to squash a lecture by Janice Fiamengo in 2013, the physical blocking of people from entering Ben Shapiro's lecture at CSULA in 2016, and the various acts of violence and vandalism at Berkeley in an outright illegal stunt to stop a College Republicans meeting. Those actions offend me, but will those who are committed to silencing others through nefarious means heed my offense and cease these strong-arm tactics? Of course they won't, and so I refuse to consider their offense whenever I am speaking about them in a negative fashion when they quite rightly deserve it.

The truth is very often uncomfortable. Who are we to tell the truth that it can't be spoken to power because it makes power feel bad about its actions? The truth is not something that can be swayed with emotion. It exists regardless of how we feel about it. The truth never goes away, and all overly sensitive people can do is force you to not acknowledge it. I decline that sinister offer entirely and so should you. This is why political discourse is in shambles at the moment, and why the entire nation appears to be shouting past itself, because we're not focusing on "truth" as the foundation of the conversation.

When we incentivize getting offended those who can make themselves appear the most offended end up with the most freedom to spread their ideas, and that is something I propose should not be stood for. That cultural reward for taking offense contributes to why so many are so determined to be offended as well, even if it runs the risk of making them appear insane. There's nothing that you can do about the types of people who will seek you out for the mere purpose of being offended and forcing you into silence. It's indicative of someone whose only interest is exercising a dirty form of power as opposed to fighting an argument on its own terms.

Now those who challenge me on this point will bring up genuine racists, sexists, Fascists, and Communists as examples of people whose ideas are just too dangerous to be allowed to speak publicly. It is proposed that they be shut down by force so their ideas don't spread. To these challengers I say that these should be your easiest targets in the realm of debate. Have we already forgotten the arguments against different flavors of bigotry and totalitarian government? Silencing these people through force or legal mandate is just going to make their ideas a forbidden fruit that more people will want to taste. All of us have experience with some authority figure telling us not to do something, and then developing a deep desire to do that very thing. A parent who violently abhors smoking is more likely to produce a child with a desire to smoke. We have two choices in front of us unless we're going to invite ourselves to be hypocrites. Either we have to take everyone's offense equally seriously, which I believe is an impossible action, or we dispense with "offense" being a factor when deliberating on whether an idea is good or bad. We are constantly being offered a "dialogue." I agree that one should take place, but I have to ask how a dialogue can take place when we don't let one side of the discussion speak.

I recognize that it's difficult to make the case for "common ground" especially to anyone who has a proclivity for the contrarian, but if there is one thing we should all agree on, it's in our freedom to disagree. There are no infallible people despite what various religions, governments, and political ideologues may tell you. Accepting that dissent should exist is winning a victory within yourself. It is accepting the most uncomfortable fact that all of us eventually have to deal with. The fact that we might be wrong.

To outlaw dissent, no matter how atrocious it might be, removes an opportunity to sharpen your arguments and removes the ability of future generations to see an argument play out. It should be a truism by now that bathing in the comfort of consensus leads to lazy thinking just as much as it is a result of it. If all we have is the conclusion we are not thinking. We must reason ourselves to a conclusion and when one decides that certain reasoning tools are not permitted, or certain avenues of thought are not permitted, then we are crippling ourselves.

To prevent dissent is to make yourself a hostage to your own opinions. If those who advocate that we encourage the suppression of offensive points of view lived in past centuries, they'd be depriving us of some of the most renowned authors in history. Thomas Paine, Henry David Thoreau, and Frederick Douglass being among them. There have been plenty of occasions in history where the dissenting party turned out to be correct after all. Not even mentioning the correctness of arguments, if we decide that opinions we think are incorrect and grotesque should be suppressed, what grounding do we have to stand on when the incorrect and grotesque gain power? How would we not be hypocrites in the face of their rule? How could we justify this right to our countrymen?

So many throughout so much of history have made the error in thinking that the solution to "dangerous speech" has been the legal strangling of that speech, but it isn't. The solution is, and always has been, more speech. Hardly anyone advocates for freedom of expression because they sympathize with some genocidal or bigoted position. They do it because if we hand over the power to regulate hatred, there is nothing stopping those we've gifted this to from deciding to regulate love. Especially if a case could be made that the general population is "offended" by it.

This attitude is not only pervasive in upper crust intellectual circles, but also in the government of the United Kingdom with the conviction and fining of Markus Meechan over the *vicious* and *unforgivable* crime of uploading a comedic YouTube video citing a draconian law that polices how offensive one can be. Adding to this scandal is the prosecution in this case remarking that context is entirely irrelevant. Since citizens of the UK have recently discovered that they live under such oppressive laws, my recommendation is for you to take your right to free speech seriously and refuse to get caught up in the permanent grey area quicksand of speech "regulation."

Do not let a law prevent you from speaking what you believe to be the truth or making a joke. Don't let the fear of arrest and prosecution padlock your mouth shut. Rights don't emerge from law. Rights emerge from what laws you are willing to break and fight against at all costs. Break whatever criminal speech law is brought down upon you. Break it often and break it with pride. Act as if you're a free person, and you will be.

## ALL'S WELLS THAT ENDS WELL

There have been science fiction works before H.G Wells existed, the major example being Frankenstein written by Mary Shelly which incorporated scientific concepts into fiction. While Frankenstein isn't scientifically accurate, it was one of the first works of fiction to replace the idea of magic with the idea of science as a plot device. It is arguable that while Mary Shelly introduced the concept of science fiction to us, H.G Wells perfected it.

There were a couple of science fiction authors like Jules Verne who wrote *Twenty Thousand Leagues Under the Sea*, and *Journey to the Center of the Earth* as well. Mary Shelly mined the ore, but H.G Wells is the one who smelted it. He's one of the key authors in defining of the science fiction genre, and he was one of the best at it. One of the reasons he was incredible at writing convincing stories of this type was because he was trained as a biologist under a contemporary of Charles Darwin.

Wells was a man of many talents and some of his first published work isn't fiction at all. They are scientific papers and commentary on science in Nature magazine. He started a diabetic research charity organization that still runs today now called "Diabetes UK." One wouldn't think he would be one of the most famous authors in history if you examined his early life first failing as a draper and then failing as a chemist's assistant, constantly going hungry. Although that's how a lot of writers start, Orwell and Bukowski among the writers who've lived difficult lives.

George Orwell was influenced by H.G Wells and they would occasionally correspond, but their personalities opposed each other in one distinct way. Orwell, when arguing, was much ruder in public than he was in private, while H.G Wells was the other way around. Orwell was writing and brought up H.G Wells like this:

*"His 'basic message' to use an expression I don't like, is that Science can solve all the ills that humanity is heir to, but that man is at present too blind to see the possibility of his own powers."*

H.G Wells then sent Orwell a personal letter filled with obscenities calling Orwell "a Trotskyist with big feet" and proceeds to object to the criticism by saying, *"I don't say that at all, read my earlier works you shit."* In case the lovely reader was curious about whether the state of public discourse is too much in disrepair.

࿐

THE ISLAND OF DOCTOR MOREAU, WHEN DISTILLED DOWN IS essentially that old trope of the hideously deformed biological experiment asking everyone to kill it, while at the same time being one of the novels in existence that exposes us to the side of our brains we try to pretend don't exist under the guise of being a horror themed *Treasure Island*. The story begins with the main character Edward Prendick shipwrecked and in a situation where he and his shipmates have to decide which person in the lifeboat to cannibalize. So he starts off in pure desperation, until he is saved by another boat carrying a bunch of animals and strange looking people. H.G Wells shines the most in this novel when he is giving gut-wrenchingly detailed descriptions of how the creatures in this story look, and when he's narrating a chase scene which happens often. He meets an scientifically educated man named Montgomery who informs him that he's headed to an island, but gives him no detail as to

68

why he is going there. Montgomery is very secretive about many things, and the main character notices that right away.

Although with all of the clues given to the reader as to what the final payoff will end up being, it becomes increasingly obvious what the horrible secret of the island is. But, due to his stellar luck, the main character gets sent adrift again and eventually lands on the island where Montgomery was headed anyhow. Provides him with food, shelter comfort, will not divulge any secrets about the island and forbids him to wander into a certain compound. Then come the screams. Prendick consistently hears screams. First it is what sounds like the puma he noticed on the ship that saved him, but then one of these screams has a certain distinct quality. The scream of a man.

He takes off pushing his way through vegetation trying to escape what he thinks will be his fate, being tortured on some kind of lab table. It's then that he discovers the Beast Men. A terrible fusion of man and beast acting out some sort of early tribal version of the human species. Pig Men appear to be performing ritual chants, some strange dark shadow creature won't stop chasing him around the island. Ape Men, Men that look like a combination of Deer and Monkey, abominations of creatures. He wretches in fear and disgust at having seen them, but after he ends up following one of the friendly Ape Men back to his den, he finds that these Beast Men have their own primitive society set up. With Laws, and a way of looking at the world, the whole nine yards. The Laws themselves are passed down to them by Dr. Moreau.

Much is talked about when it comes to "playing God" and there's the idea that humanity is arrogant for suggesting that mere sentient intelligent life is the highest sentient power in the Universe presently acting on it. But here's the thing, what if we are? What if there is no "God" to play? HG Wells believed in Darwin's Theory of Evolution back when it actually took a big set of gonads to believe in Darwin's Theory of Evolution publicly. In the book Moreau not only experiments on these poor creatures, but after dumbing them down infects them with a kind of religion that lifts himself to the position of a deity. The Laws were instituted so that the "animal side" of the Beast Men wouldn't take over, and all of the Laws are followed by the desperate phrase "Are we not men?" and the answer to that question is quite obviously nobody knows. But the Laws read as follows:

1. Not to go on all fours
2. Not to suck up Drink
3. Not to eat Flesh nor Fish
4. Not to claw bark of trees
5. Not to chase other Men

The man/animal hybrids on the island were convinced that they were human. Perhaps, representative of the inability for the society in which H.G Wells lived to accept the idea that humans are indeed animals despite their best efforts to avoid that fact. But that's just one person's interpretation. What is immediately apparent to me is the satirical look at religion as well with its ritual chants, and Laws that aren't really thought about but are passed down by what is perceived to be a higher power that demands you outrage your true nature. But then again, is it not in our nature to defy our nature? The more you think about the themes and message of this book the more you think that humanity's very existence is a walking contra-diction.

While some may view this book as sort of a dystopian warning when it comes to what ethic-less science is capable of and I understand where they are coming from absolutely. You can read that determination on the back of the version of the book that includes the "Modern Library Reading Guide" in it. But I disagree with that interpretation not because it is wrong, but perhaps because it is incomplete. I see it as a commentary on humanity's inability to fully accept its animal nature. Espe-cially when you couple this book with Wells' education as a biologist and his belief in the theory of evolution. And you blend that with the various distorted hybrid creatures being insistent that "none escape" this fate while at the same time being insistent that they are Men. Plus the fact that the main character was shipwrecked, saved, and then set out adrift a second time, AND the main character Prendick would rather drown himself than become like the Beast Men.

It's pretty clear what Wells was trying to express to us. The main idea brought forth in the book is that there are both good and bad sides to humanity's animal nature, and we need to be vigilant in embracing the good and combating the bad. Dr. Moreau is a symbol of science without ethics, and a disregarding of pain. Dr. Moreau is essentially torturing these animals both physically and mentally by trying to turn them into men by dissecting them and rearranging them. You get Dr. Moreau when you abandon your humanity altogether and when there's reasoning that doesn't consider empathy and compassion important. You hear this in his explanation, after his horrific practice is discovered by the main character, when he says this:

*"You see, I went on with this research just the way it led me. That is the only way I ever heard of research going. I asked a question, devised some method of getting an answer, and got...a fresh question. Was this possible, or that possible? You cannot imagine what this means to an investigator, what an intellectual passion grows upon him. You cannot imagine the strange colorless delight of these intellectual desires. The thing before you is no longer an animal, a fellow-creature, but a problem. Sympathetic pain, all I know of it I remember as a thing I used to suffer from years ago. I wanted, it was the only thing I wanted, to find out the extreme limit of plasticity in a living shape. To this day I have never troubled about the ethics of the matter. The study of Nature makes a man at last as remorseless as Nature. I have gone on, not heeding anything but the question I was pursuing, and the material has dripped into the huts yonder."*

No empathy. He does not care about the consequences of his actions. He is principally concerned about the next puzzle and how to solve it, regardless of what actions he must take to find it out. An abandoning of the good side of animal nature that has been evolved into us. Dr. Moreau is a symbol of both ethic-less science, and the idea that biology is inescapable. Considering no matter how hard he tries he can't turn beasts into rational creatures. Eventually the animal sides of the

Beast Men get the better of them, as it always seems to. And there's lots of death.

There's not much difference between the creatures he discovers and the ancient societies of man. Apart from the fact that they are all a disfigured melding of present day animal. The main character also relates the Beast Men to regular men after returning to wider society. If anything, H.G Wells was trying to get across that humans are at bottom, animals. Without any specific value judgment being placed on that fact. While we are unique as animals, we are animals nonetheless. A difficult thing to sell when this book was published too.

The book was published 40 years after Charles Darwin published his "Origin of Species." People at that time were still relatively unwilling to accept the conclusion that humans evolve to adapt to their environment just like any animal does. As humans are not divinely special in the eyes of the Universe. Humans are unique as an animal, but not to the point of ascension out of our biology, right? The environment molded us, but we also were eventually able to mold our environment when it didn't suit us, to a much greater extent than any other animal could dream of doing. The environment molded us to mold it.

I hope I'm not personifying the environment too much for your tastes, but hopefully you get what I'm trying to get across here. We can mold our environment, but what if we eventually develop the technology that allows us to mold our biology. Not in the sense of medicine, or growing ears on lab rats, but the ability to shape the DNA of our offspring down to the last detail? Does molding our environment, thus altering positive survival traits, thus guiding the natural process of evolution in certain directions, constitute humans already intentionally molding their biology? One can't really separate the environment that humans evolve to adapt into, and their biology. One is necessarily dependent on the other. Humans will continue to evolve and if I could live long enough to see it, it would be very interesting especially considering the various environments we've constructed for ourselves.

Telling an uncomfortable truth via a story. I've always had respect for that. Man hardly ever wants to take a glimpse at the animal side of himself. One doesn't need to embrace the animal side of oneself to recognize that it's there. By "animal nature" I'm speaking of something like "unthinking instinct" or us trying to intellectually and morally justify our unthinking instincts. I can separate the ideas of natural and bad obviously. Something can be natural and be good like empathy, although that can have downsides as well were it to be taken advantage of. Just because we know that we are animals and are subject to the same laws of nature as any other creature doesn't mean we have to revert back to some uncivilized animal state of being. Just because we've reached a level of civilization that's relatively peaceful considering the entirety of the past doesn't mean we've grown out of our animal need for tribalism and superstition. I do think that those things are worth growing out of. It doesn't seem to be something that people are willing to give up just yet. It snowballs out of control too doesn't it? If you don't feel a special connection to those of your race, your sex, your occupation, your countrymen, those who have the same political opinions as you, biological data and statistical averages aren't going to convince you to feel those things, nor are those things necessary for you to feel. Tribal forces always justify themselves through the existence of opposing tribal forces without fail. When confronted with the choice between truth and victory people will pretty much always choose victory. When confronted with the choice between right-eousness and survival people will pretty much always choose survival.

Why do you think the biggest and most dangerous lies ever told have to do with you and everyone you love being on the precipice of death and suffering? It immediately activates the animal within us, and turns our moral compass into a wheel of fortune. You can't get a large group of humans to kill innocent people by just proposing it outright, we have empathy evolved into us, you need to convince them that those innocent people are causing you and your loved ones intense suffering by their existence. That they don't deserve empathy. All of that is just taking advantage of our animal nature. It wouldn't work if we didn't have a bad side to our animal nature. It's partly why we see historical patterns of empire, subjugation, and revolution.

When we embrace the animal side of ourselves we stop seeing civilization as a useful exercise in itself and depending on how you've divided the tribes up, or have had the lines drawn for you, nearly everyone in the out-group is a threat. However, when we pretend it isn't there it gets taken advantage of. The outcome of both of those states of affairs would be completely negative. I can see no positive aspect of either of those attitudes. That's partly the point H.G Wells was trying to make in this book, and it's a point that I'm inclined to agree with. That animal nature while inescapable due to us being animals is at least worth examining and questioning.

What makes us unique animals is that we have the ability to examine and question ourselves. One can't disagree about the facts when they are proven beyond a reasonable doubt to be true, but one can always disagree about what one does in response to said facts. The figure of Dr. Moreau, while being a warning of the ethical problems that may come from the discoveries of Darwin, also reveals that the truth of the matter here which is that there isn't much separation between man and beast. But what little that does separate man from beast should be protected and amplified as opposed to drowned out in favor of letting our animal side take hold of us. Who knows? This could just be a creepy story about a mad scientist.

# DO YOU TAKE YOUR COFFEE
# WITH PROGRESS?

I live in an area that was once considered a "rough part of town" by Massachusetts standards, but recently the place has been spruced up and a cavalcade of college students moved in. Two men were shot dead a week ago at around 1AM on the street next to mine. When I woke up the day after there was torn crime scene tape on the ground, then when I returned home the NBC news van was still scoping out the area. Around the same distance in the opposite direction is a large billboard advertising some kind of organic plant milk that reads: "Do You Take Your Coffee With Progress?"

There's a gem of dark irony there that my mediocre vocabulary can't quite mine yet. Everyone I knew and respected got horrifically political during and after the 2016 election. It's become next to impossible to avoid. Political creep is a very dangerous beast and it should be shunned back into its proper place as often as possible. As someone interested in staying informed about the state of the world though I have to subject myself to the gauntlet of journalistic malpractice, vapid politics, dishonest sloganeering, general incivility, and cults of personality currently thriving in the mid-2010s. Politics has become a replica of Reality TV for those who consider themselves above such mindless programming. Despite the

tantrums that are thrown on the daily by "analysts," the
United States deserves the President it has.

To cement us in time, Justice Kennedy just retired and a
meltdown ensued over the inevitable conservative dominated
Supreme Court. Before his Nixonian "strike back" instinct
subsided, Trump posted a Tweet wherein he gloated about his
stellar writing capabilities. Citing the many wonderful books
he has written hitting the "Fake News Media" back for
mocking his tendency to capitalize for emphasis, presumably
forgetting that he hired Tony Schwartz as a ghostwriter. A
group of self-righteous slothy opportunistic journalists had to
walk back a condemnation of Trump after discovering pictures
of children locked in cages were taken during Obama's time in
office. A mass of Trump sycophants demanded that he receive
the Nobel Peace Prize for preventing nuclear war in the
Korean peninsula despite the fact that North Korea has shown
no sign of denuclearization thus far.

This is all standing on the foundation of a nationwide
debate over whether being civil with each other about political
matters is tantamount to complicity in the perpetration of
evil. This is a cross-section of the moronic world Americans
currently live in that will be filtered out of history in about five
decades. This overbearing culture of stupid hip-fire filler
content was taking its toll on me, and I needed to quit politics
for a while. I started treating it like fast food, or as if I was in a
rehab center for politics addicts. Everything in moderation
they say. Being just another punch in the mosh-pit was out of
the question.

It was just after Pride Month and just before
Independence Day when I took a small trip around New
England trying to clear my mind of all this nonsense. On the
way up to New Hampshire there were signs littering the
highway reminding Massachusetts residents that fireworks are
illegal in their state. Clearly a cautionary measure against only
the most jelly-like spines. Part of me thinks these laws are just

another piece of the Independence Day celebration. The government knows its police officers won't enforce a law against fireworks on a day where their use is to commemorate the abolition of government tyranny.

Oftentimes, when answering a fireworks related noise complaint, the police will bring their cruiser around, shut the lights off, watch the show until the finale, then pretend to ask the crowd questions about what happened and give the host a reluctant talking to as if it matters. No one is getting arrested or fined for fireworks on Independence Day, because if they did not only would it subject every American citizen to mind-crushing irony, but it would also make the police department look like a bunch of authoritarian buzzkills who might as well be operating in the name of the Crown. The next day that same officer might shoot one of those audience members for reaching for their wallet too fast on a traffic stop.

I noticed a flag I'd never seen before waving in the warm summer breeze. It was a black and white version of the Stars and Stripes with a thin blue line cutting the flag in half horizontally. I was told that it is supposed to commemorate police officers killed in the line of duty. Almost every pick-up truck on the road was outfitted with an American Flag. One over-weight motorcyclist stuck three upright flags into the rear of his machine. An American flag was dead center and flying the highest, to the left was the standard black "Remember Prisoners of War" flag, to the right flew a Gadsden flag bearing the famous words "Don't Tread On Me."

"They sure take 'Live Free or Die' seriously up here don't they?" I thought.

That damn billboard kept creeping up in my memory. "Progress" has always been a word I've despised due to how politicians use it. Often when there is some big meeting or ongoing problem and the American people are clamoring for an update what is offered to them is the vague phrase, "Progress has been made." It is a complete omission of anything tangible. It says nothing about what has been done, how it has been done, or why it was done. The phrase itself relies on the listener to insert whatever they consider to be "progress" into the statement. It's no wonder that advertisers have seized upon the vagueness of political language in order to sell products. People don't just want to buy a decent product, they want to feel like they are performing a moral good by purchasing a product too.

❦

After I was done with New Hampshire I high-tailed it down to Provincetown. On the way into the town sand dunes lined the highway and they were dotted with varying shades of green circling a small body of agitated salt-water. There were cyclists clogging up the road and so I was determined to figure out what they were doing.

My first experience in the town was being screamed at by someone in a portable toilet. I had to use the bathroom, it said it was occupied but the door looked open. I knocked on the door a couple of times and a man aggressively roared from the inside, "What, what do you want?"

"Ok," I said passive aggressively and began walking down the street.

"Ya know, it's not my fault you shit yourself, buddy!" I shouted as soon as I was confident in my ability to escape if he chased after me. It's not like he could run very fast with shorts full of his own filth anyhow.

As I walked through the streets I saw people wearing tight shirts, pretty much everyone sporting a pair of sunglasses, psychic readings, jewelry stores, small restaurants and cafes, an old man wearing a sleeveless shirt that read "Citizen of the World" on it, another man smoking a massive cigar with a Marine Corps shirt on. I guarantee the two people I mentioned would absolutely despise one another based on their apparel and attitude in conversation, but I tried my best to avoid judging books by covers. I see displays like this the same way I see someone wearing a Harley-Davidson shirt, or a hoodie from some nearby college. Walking advertisements.

The world of politics and advertising are so close to one another that they can be pretty much be classed as the same field, because one isn't a "successful politician" if they think things through enough and come to the decent conclusions. We consider someone a "successful politician" when they can convince enough people to do something. Just like in the advertising industry. You don't necessarily need a stellar product to be successful in business. You just need to convince enough people to buy it. Hence, why political campaigns aren't anything more than glorified marketing efforts forced down our throats. What one has to rebuff is the ever creeping narcissistic tendency that everyone except for oneself does things for superficial or dubious reasons. For all I know this man was in a rush to get out of the house and threw on whatever he could grab.

I walked into a restaurant and sat at the bar. I ordered a Corona because I didn't have much money, I was told everything out here was expensive, and I needed to hydrate and deal with my innate fear of crowds somehow. An old couple, already both drunk in the afternoon, insisted on buying my first beer despite my repeated refusal. I didn't even need to ask the question, but they explained to me that the cyclists were part of a charity event for those with Multiple Sclerosis, somberly adding that their daughter suffered from the disease. They eventually filed out of the bar after bombarding me with stories about their personal lives, and bragging about having twenty-two grandchildren. It wasn't that I was uninterested in their stories, it's that they wouldn't let me speak too and I was trying to release the negativity brought about by that guy in the porta-potty.

I had another Corona and then left the bar, hoping to find something interesting to do. This didn't happen. One of my trip-mates insisted that I take care of their dog while they got a tattoo, so I tried to walk the thing down to the beach for a minute, but he ended up getting aggressive with every dog he saw and peed on a perfectly innocent baby's stroller.

I was far too angry and frustrated to deal with this goddamn town anymore and so I insisted on leaving. On the way back to the car I pounded on the wall of the rogue toilet hoping that guy was still sitting there so I could give him a piece of my mind. I got no response. There was no reasonable reason for me to do something like that either, and I might have frightened a perfectly innocent person trying to relieve themselves. Then they would get angry after a few hours in this town and leave, but not before also taking their anger out on a mobile bathroom.

I'M NOT PROUD OF CONTRIBUTING TO THE CYCLE OF negativity, but I'd be a liar if I said I never contribute. This judgmental attitude of mine was just a lingering aftereffect of the "Culture War" in the mid-2010s which is still an ongoing cycle of negativity. Not constructive negativity either, but sour and nasty stuff. I've spoken to numerous activists within different brackets of the political spectrum, and despite all of their moral grandstanding some of them are very malicious people. Especially the younger ones who consider themselves to be on the front lines exorcising dangerous subversive political elements from the United States. One activist told me that he knows of people who disguise themselves as the opposition, act like they are just there for the protesting, and cause trouble so that it stokes bad press for their opponents. He followed this revelation up with a hearty chuckle.

Some from the "young activist" class display that chest-puffing personality that says things like, "I swear if one of those fuckers gets up in my face I'll break their jaw." They giggle to themselves about the thought of breaking someone else's nose in a fistfight despite the innocent face they display to the camera after the brawl ends, arrests are made, and everyone cools down. If given the option to de-escalate or escalate a situation, these young activist types will pretty much always choose to escalate it and then use the inevitable violence as another reason for why they need to be violent in the future.

It's not so much a quest to expose the truth and have better policy implemented as much as it is a watered down version of political gang warfare where every single person has a long list of personal grievances that only a good right hook can solve for them. This type of thing has already ended in multiple deaths in the United States. These flashes of activist violence I mean. The journalists can't get a handle on it because none of them want to speak to them for fear of either being beaten up, or for fear that the elements they've been tacitly cheering on behind their computers are far more violent than they anticipated. One wouldn't be able to tell that this type of thing was happening if they didn't talk to them personally, and instead spent their time in cute gift shops buying "citizen of the world" merchandise.

In the context of Pride Month and Patriotism, hardly any of these activists would celebrate both of these things. They each consider one of those holidays to be annoying, blind, mindless, or at worst harmful. I suppose this isn't so much a cycle as it is a downward spiral. The cultures of smug radical chic and obnoxious country bumpkin collided like two enormous asteroids that have circled one another for decades and not even I could escape the gravity.

I TRIED TO CLEAR MY HEAD OF ALL OF THIS AS I SHOT OVER to Martha's Vineyard. The women there wore flowing summer dresses if they were over 35, anyone under 35 would almost certainly be in what is colloquially called a "denim thong." Extremely tiny jean shorts and a tight shirt. The men there wore largely the same things regardless of age. A collared shirt and shorts. I blended in well.

I ended up at a place where Margaritas were the specialty beverage and I ordered one. The fake smiles of the staff were easy to see through. They would disappear instantly whenever they turned away from a customer, and sometimes they wouldn't return when taking another order. I could understand their frustration completely. I'd be pissed if I had to serve people like this day in and day out too. The pinnacle of upper-middle class America. A yipping pack of New England socialites. Not so rich that they can buy their own island, but they have enough money to frequently travel to someone else's. Filled with all of the resentment of the lower classes scoffing at the sizes of some of the privately owned boats, yet still having plenty of room for snootiness when presented with a lowly waiter or waitress. Nope, I was getting political again. Judgmental. Compartmentalizing like this isn't healthy but my gut was usually right when it came to the interpersonal.

One staff member brought a round to a table of young women.

"Here you are, Strawberry Margarita, Gin and Tonic, Vodka soda, and a Classic Margarita" the staff member said.

"Um, I ordered mine without salt on the rim. I hate to ask, but would you mind making it again?" the Classic Margarita girl said.

"Oh, I'm sorry. I'll fix that." The staff member replied as she took the drink away.

Turning to her friends once the staff member was out of earshot the customer giggled, "How fucking hard is it to remember a drink order?" Her friends supported her comment with a chorus of "I know, ugh."

I had been vindicated. I was looking for something, and I wasn't quite sure what the story here was. I could write about how duplicity was alive and well, but everyone knows that already. My inner cynic was screaming about how this was just a poorly narrated vacation across New England in the middle of two holidays.

What always pushed itself forward was the image of that billboard looming over two dead men in the middle of the street. The image of the NBC van lingering around my apartment. I was imagining "citizen of the world" guy and "USMC" guy exchanging pleasantries during a business transaction, but then having a shouting match about immigration policy over social media under the guise of anonymous accounts. People tend to see themselves as either the center of attention, whether positive or negative, or completely invisible. In reality it's somewhere in-between. You're usually just a passing observation. In a nation full of judgmental people watchers, we all eventually end up getting looked at.

Whenever a generation hits twenty-five they begin struggling to define themselves historically. A nationwide identity crisis begins to take form. I'm in the middle of an age-defining "Culture War" I am told. Within these "Culture Wars" everything takes on a partisan flavor. Art, business, science, journalism, etc. One can't enjoy anything for its own sake. It must be enjoyed for the appropriate political reasons. Those who are addicted to politics can't keep their habit to themselves anymore. They must inflict it on others. Over the past few years it is true that I contributed to this mess. I obsessed over politics and joined the arena for a long time. I was rude when I shouldn't have been, ignorant when I shouldn't have been, and arrogant when it was anything but necessary.

However, I would do it all over again were I given the opportunity. Friends were made. Enemies were crushed. Scars were received. Wounds inflicted. Minds washed. Mind made dirty again. Unnecessary and necessary anger. The strongest comradery outside of the military and sports teams.

There was something about watching all of those company logos flickering on tall buildings retreat over the horizon when leaving Boston. Watching the tall abandoned cranes fly by. The clouds were painted in the sky with large white brush strokes. People setting off, people returning home, people unsure of their destination. Phones all out gently illuminating the faces with an off-white sheen. The crinkling of bags. The sound of ice knocking together in a plastic cup. In a comfortable state between sleep and full awareness. All the while surrounded by two sweet delicate false ideas. The idea that I'd leave it all behind now, and the idea that I was nothing like anyone I'd observed over the past two years of my life.

# A PROPOSAL: REVIVE "THE NEW
JOURNALISM"

Bring your imagination forward and picture two cliffs over-
looking a deep dark canyon. Over which is a thin taut
tightrope. One of these ledges represents dry reporting typi-
fied by old black and white television and radio news with all
of its faults and benefits. It doesn't allow for a coloring of the
facts and sticks strictly to reporting on what can be objectively
proven like the number of soldiers in a garrison and the
content of conversations. Pure untarnished observations from
the perspective of someone without a dog in the fight. The use
of fanciful language is seized upon and strangled for fear of
provoking an avoidable emotional response from the
consumer. The writing is very technical and direct much like a
lab report or a set of instructions for assembling some piece of
junk furniture. On this ridge journalism is treated like a
science complete with its own method of data collection,
confirmation, and strict rigid rules of presentation. The adjec-
tive is almost non-existent here unless it is necessary for
context within the report. It is fact-driven and avoids contro-
versy. Even attempting to inch one's way into creative and
"harsh but accurate" language use is considered "editorializ-
ing." Outright calling a President a "liar" is out of the question
in this realm of journalism. Respect reigns supreme. It is
boring, stale, and consuming it is more of a chore than

anything else. Not many truly *want* to consume this type of program, but some think that we must lest we rot in an ever-growing sea of our own fact-less grime. They have it correct, to a degree. They value the right things in the profession of journalism, but the dull nature of the presentation and obsession with appearing respectable completely halts any kind of business success or reach. If no one is reading the truth you've given, how informed are they?

The cliff on the other side of the ravine represents a kind of journalism where creativity and "spreading a message" is the main focal point. Contemporary and online-only rags stand by this system. The language use is extravagant and there is no terror in forcing words like, "awful, horrific, vicious, sleazy, joyful, ratbag, scumbucket, corrupt and disgusting" into the foreground. Facts are abandoned if they don't fit the structure of the argument the journalist is making, or the story that they are trying to tell. It is very story oriented, and the line between fact and fiction is all but invisible. What is commonly called "clickbait" resides on this side of the gorge. The business savvy, political opportunists and outright propagandists make their home on this cliff. The type that "isn't afraid to tell it like it is" despite being completely unsure of "what is." The type that proclaims loudly that objectivity is impossible and facts are meant to be interpreted, not observed.

This is where the "cable news roundtable analysts" are. Most of them are completely useless creatures that only exist to push a campaign, boot-lick the present Administration, or rabble-rouse about a "wave of pushback" or a "revolution." Success is not predicated on the truth-value of the words, but on the political impact they have or how many become convinced of the arguments. Creativity and literary technique flourish, but facts become road blocks as opposed to necessary components. While they don't much care for reality they certainly know how to draw a crowd and take advantage of the advertiser-based free for all that the Internet has turned news into.

This dilemma has plagued journalists since someone first tried to relay information, but overall it is a false choice. The twenty-four hour news cycle has eviscerated nearly every shred of credibility that cable news had left. When one needs to fill up twenty-four hours of the day with hot exciting news, one finds that they must sensationalize, repeat, and have predictable partisan discussions about various news items. There is an ingrained cultural feeling in America that "news" and "journalism" must come from the radio, television, newspapers, and now online publications.

What we no longer seem to value is long-form journalism delivered via book. In order to illicit both understanding from the consumer and well-rounded accuracy in reporting, one must spend a lot of time immersing themselves in the story and books give the journalist the opportunity to do such a thing. Newspapers have all sorts of restrictions on what they will print, what a journalist is allowed to say, and in how many words they have to say it. Some of the greatest reporting of the 20$^{th}$ Century was done through books.

*Hell's Angels* was written by Hunter S. Thompson after spending a little over a year embedded in one of the motor-cycle gang's chapters during a time when the nation was in an uproar about them, and mainstream newspapers would do no more than the passing interview. *Homage to Catalonia* should be required reading for anyone attempting to dive into the Spanish Civil War or journalism in general. Anyone interested in 60s drug culture would be remiss if they didn't read *The Electric Kool-Aid Acid Test*.Whoever wants to explore WWI should immediately pick up a copy of *Storm of Steel*.

These weren't works of "partisanship," nor were these merely dry lists of facts. These were written by people who put themselves through the ringer and came out with a story on the other side. These writers were able to properly inform readers about what was going on because they were there. They experienced it themselves. There is only so much jour-nalism that can be done behind a keyboard that isn't a copy-paste job using other journalistic outfits as sources or scanning social media for something or other. Journalism has been bogged down by complication in recent years with tired philo-sophical questions when the answer to "what journalism is" is simpler than determining what color the sky is on any given day.

When boiled down, journalism is the art of relaying infor-mation and explaining things. Anyone who told their friends about that time they almost got hit in an intersection has "done journalism" using the broadest possible definition of the word itself. Was it good journalism? Listed in order of impor-tance that depends on how accurately the story was relayed, how informed the listener was by the story, and how enter-tained the listener was by the story. Some journalists scoff at the idea of entertaining their readers. I was part of that school of thought once too. But one can't simply dismiss that aspect of reporting with how sparse attention has become.

"The New Journalism" blends literature and journalism into one giant shapeless globule that manages to employ the best parts of both fields in the service of informing the public. This freewheeling style allows the journalist to insert their opinion without distorting the facts. It provides a license for literary technique, using it for the expressed purpose of getting people *interested* in the truth. The genre is volatile and unstable by its very nature, and there is nothing stopping someone making use of this method in order to spread lies. Either that or deciding that the literary and artistic merit of the piece takes precedence over the "fact of the matter." This, while it makes wonderful art and literature, cannot be entirely trusted to inform the populace. What if it were possible to write non-fiction novels that valued the truth over literary and artistic merit, but still permitted the use of themes, beautiful language, and suspense? Is it possible to write a "good story" about "the truth" without sacrificing either for the sake of the other?

The examples I have given above should support the argu-ment that it is indeed possible, although not easy. It requires months to years of dedicated embedding, observation, inter-viewing, experiencing, and writing. Journalists and writers of all stripes have been doing it for centuries, but only recently have we witnessed a decline in supporters of this method. We've relegated ourselves to browsing the news when we're bored on social media, skimming standard-less online tabloids, and buying subscriptions to restricting mainstream papers. It's as if we've decided as a society that journalism must either be boring and prudish, or filled with lies and hackery. This is a choice that I refuse to accept, and it's a choice that future journalists should reject as well. May the era of the "nonfiction novel" flourish once more! The age of artistic and journalistic independence is here and gatekeeping is nearly impossible. Take advantage of it. All it takes is a little bit of interest, a hearty dose of dedication, and an unflinching desire to explain the world accurately and beautifully.

Journalism *can* be literature. Literature *can* be Journalism. Not only can art imitate life, it can report on it too. It's a delicate balance, walking that tightrope across the two platforms of pure dry stuffy objectivity and fact-distorting emotional fanfare. But if one can do it successfully without leaning too much to one side and plummeting into the eternal chasm of failure, the view, I can guarantee, is much more valuable, memorable, and true than anything the current state of journalism and literature can offer us at present.

# ACKNOWLEDGMENTS

Thank you to Sarah, Tyler, Nicholas, and my parents.

# ABOUT THE AUTHOR

Photo by @VoxProvidence

Justin Little is an independent writer and journalist based out of Massachusetts. He reports using "New Journalism," a dying form brought into prominence during the sixties and seventies. He has reported on the 2017 Boston Free Speech Rally, various other young activist events, and has spoken to college students in El Paso. He has been posting his ramblings online since 2015 and has amassed around 80,000 subscribers on YouTube. His influences include but are not limited to George Orwell, Hunter S. Thompson, Tom Wolfe, Christopher Hitchens, Ernest Hemingway, and Ray Bradbury. Most of his time is spent planning future journalistic escapades, reading and reviewing books, and pacing around searching for something useful to say.

Jeff Burk

## HE HAS MANY NAMES
Drew Chial

## CENOTE CITY
Monique Quintana

## THIS BOOK AIN'T NUTTIN TO FUCK WITH: A WU-TANG TRIBUTE ANTHOLOGY
edited by Christoph Paul & Grant Wamack

# CLASH

WE PUT THE **LIT** IN LITERARY

CPSIA information can be obtained
at www.ICGtesting.com
Printed in the USA
BVHW082022131118
532961BV00003B/413/P

9 781944 866259